damien coulthard & rebecca sullivan

forewords by bruce pascoe & dale tilbrook

warndu mai
good food

introducing native australian ingredients to your kitchen

hachette
AUSTRALIA

Contents

Foreword by Bruce Pascoe

Australia's history can be told through food. We ate mutton, and mutton, more mutton, and we ate it with potatoes. The cuisine of England. Later we ate Chinese because, even though the country distanced itself from the Asian goldminers, the food was fresh and flavourful. Each new wave of migration had us eating Indian, Italian, Greek, Vietnamese and African foods. Anything but Australian.

Cook your way through this book but remember that you can't eat our Aboriginal food if you can't swallow our history. Here are the ingredients of your country. Enjoy them in these recipes and prepare yourselves for the flours and tubers that will follow them, the staple foods that grew hundreds of generations of Australians.

Australian Aboriginal people domesticated, cooked and cared for foods which are adapted to our country's climate and fertility. Most of those foods are perennial and sequester carbon; handy attributes in a drying climate. And we did it for around 100,000 years. In the process we invented bread 65,000 years ago. A difficult piece of news to deliver to the French!

One day a government will pay Australian farmers to grow these foods simply for the purpose of saving the planet. The old people grew these foods in a deliberate plan to care and sustain. Throw yourself into these flavours and acknowledge the glorious fact that they come from your country, no other. This is the start of an Australian cuisine. We are not a Vegemite sandwich, we are Australian. Let's eat our country's food.

Bruce Pascoe
Yuin man, writer

Foreword by Dale Tilbrook

Bush food, bush tucker, Australian native edibles. Many names for what was essentially our traditional food before European settlement. Except that it was always more than just food. It is still our totems, our connection to country, our medicine. It demands of us conservation, collaboration and reverence.

This was how Aboriginal Australia operated before European settlement. We grew, we harvested, we collected, we thrived. It is hard to do that now. Most urban Aboriginal people would be hard-pressed to find access to traditional food in any meaningful quantities except perhaps for kangaroo meat.

However, as the bush food industry has grown, there have been opportunities to buy more plant foods. Wattleseed, lemon myrtle and anise myrtle, pepperberries and pepperleaf, saltbush and other native herbs. Mostly used as flavourings rather than functional foods because of price and availability. It is still a fledgling industry and as exposure grows through use by chefs on TV cooking shows (we know you watch them – we all do), more and more ordinary folk want to incorporate something from the bush into their cooking. Nurseries have begun to offer bush food plants. This is great, because growing your own supplies at home is the way to go, or buying them commercially. Laws will vary from state to state but it's unlikely you are legally able to go out and forage or wild harvest if it is not your country, except on private land.

Of course, early settlers had no such restrictions and they gathered, used and created classics that are still favourites today: rosella jam, quandong jam; they also utilised the native greens to keep their families healthy and relished the access to good quality meat – kangaroo.

As more European food became available, many native foods were consigned again to the bush and forgotten, until the recent resurgence of interest. But not by us. We still gathered and ate, hunted and burnt until our numbers dwindled, our access to land was restricted and our wonderful crops overrun by sheep, cattle and ignorance. Other people tell this part of our history far more eloquently than I.

Yet somehow all was not lost. There is still a great deal of knowledge amongst Aboriginal people and others about the bounty of the bush. The great yam gardens along the Swan River in Perth may have all but vanished, but there is still a remnant to see at Walyunga National Park. The rainforests of Queensland are still flush with an amazing diversity of tropical fruits and in South Australia a robust quandong industry exists. Sandalwood nuts are enjoying a new status as a local tree nut that overtakes macadamia nuts for health benefits (more protein and dietary fibre and a similar amount of mono-unsaturated fats). Wattleseed graces the pages of this and every bush food recipe book for its roasted coffee, mocha and hazelnut flavours. Small cakes were made from wattleseed flour; high in protein, iron and zinc, these little treasures replenished lean, healthy bodies. These were our foods, medicine and life force.

Things change. No society stands still. But the knowledge, the intellectual property is held by us, the First Nations peoples of Australia. It would be wonderful to think that, moving forward, this is acknowledged. Benefit-sharing makes sense, in our old ways, and today.

Dale Tilbrook
Wardandi Bibbulmun Yok

A Note from Damien

One of my fondest memories is of visiting my grandparents in Nepabunna, Flinders Ranges as a child. My introduction to culture was not evident from the start. Those visits always included seeing significant places, moving across country and, almost always, picking and eating fresh urti (quandong).

It was in these spots that I remember hearing family members sharing stories. Often in language. Even though I didn't understand Adnyamathanha, I remember the stories because of where we were and what surrounded us. The vast sprawling Flinders Ranges. Created by my ancestral beings.

The stories then didn't really mean all that much, but now, they mean everything. I have become connected to my culture more than ever and one of the reasons this has happened is because of Warndu.

Let me tell you how Warndu came about.

Connection to family is the most important thing to me. It is something that has been taught to me from as early as I can remember: family comes first.

Food is always the glue. In any family. In mine it was camping on country. Sitting together and eating. Pop would find things like witchetty grubs and nori (sweet sap that grows on the acacia trees). He would share them with us and with that came a story that was from his childhood.

Pop's childhood was vastly different to mine. He grew up in a time where the transition from living in a traditional world to living in a western world was forced. Elders of the community, both male and female, were governed in every aspect of life including the passing on of story, language, food and traditional ways. Such experiences have caused intergenerational trauma, to not just my Adnyamathanha nation, but all Aboriginal nations across Australia.

Although these experiences are in the past, Aboriginal communities have stayed resilient and strong by maintaining their identity through as simple a thing as the food they eat.

Food as we all know is a powerful tool. Its nostalgic power, its ability to promote curiosity and question and most importantly its story relating to place or provenance as we would call it today. Every single food source to my people has a story dating back thousands and thousands of years. From the red kangaroo to the Urti. This is not just food; this is our creation, our story, our tradition, us.

Recently I was on the Amalfi coast. We visited a winery with some friends and as I listened to the group's absolute excitement over a 500-year-old vine from which the wine they were drinking originated, I was astonished. It made me think: Australians get excited at the thought of a 500-year-old vine. Yet here is my food, 60,000-plus years old, and no one seems to hold any excitement for any of it – any of the thousands and thousands of nuts, seeds, plants and proteins.

Warndu was created out of necessity. Because I want people to have that same excitement for our foods as they did for the age of that vine. Because when my pop was diagnosed with dementia, I knew those campfire stories would stop, that food would stop, that source of culture and language would stop, and in an instant another chapter of Aboriginal narrative is lost.

We hope to share these amazing foods with all Australians, so they can taste the flavours of my backyard. To feel like they too are out in those ranges, around that campfire or simply sitting with family sharing stories.

A Note from Rebecca

My 'aha!' moment hit me like a slap in the face. Here I was, a local food advocate for the best part of ten years, and I hadn't even tried anything truly local to my own country. My own backyard. To my embarrassment, I realised that local food surely must be the Australian native plants and animals. And so my true local food journey began.

I met my partner, Damien in 2013. My work is all about 'granny skills' and protecting our elders' knowledge and heritage. In Damien's culture that is of the utmost importance, too. History is orally recorded, not written. When Damien's pop was diagnosed with dementia, that was when Damien really realised what was being lost, and the importance of the work I was doing also.

Everyone eats. Food prompts curiosity, and sitting around a table is a safe place. When we host anything from dinner parties to pop-up restaurants and share these new flavours with people they ask questions and those questions lead to conversations, not just about food but also about culture and history, heritage and story.

That's when we decided to start our own company (which has evolved into a food, wellbeing and educational brand),

Warndu, which means 'good' in Damien's Adnyamathanha language. We pride ourselves on championing Australian native foods and teaching people as much as we can through what we have learnt in the past few years creating food products so that some of this information is not lost forever. We truly believe food is the pathway to change.

The most important thing about this book is that we are really taking the role of home education seriously. We are not chefs, just home cooks. We are not doctors, so anything relating to health and medicine comes purely from our own opinions and experience. We are not horticulturists, so what we've learnt about plants has come from family, friends and industry experts. We are passing on only what we have had permission to do so in a culturally respectful way. We believe that although we are championing native foods and want to see a thriving industry, the intellectual property of all of these foods must always remain with our nation's first people. That is something that is being worked on by many different groups of people and industries. It is a complex issue and we among many others are working hard to find a positive outcome for all in the near future.

The Australian native food industry has had its ups and downs and, like all trends, seen great successes. But it can't just be a trend, it needs to be the norm. Without it trickling down to the home, it will never be a sustainable industry. Native food needs to be in every pantry in every home in Australia. Our people need it, our farmers need it, our country needs it and our soil needs it.

There are many incredible Indigenous harvesters, growers, producers, farmers, chefs, food businesses big and small and champions in this industry. Chefs who have always championed these foods (not just for a month then given up on them when they realise it's hard to get supply) have made these foods their entire menu and not just a garnish for token's sake. The growers, harvesters and distributors of native foods who have been doing it for decades are the real heroes. They are the grafters. Many of them have been working their asses off for many years before us, working so hard they have burnt themselves out, fighting for a cause – a bloody good one. They put in the hard work, and we are now just trying to do them proud, to collaborate and learn from everyone. Food is powerful and can create curiosity and conversation. In that we create demand, and a sustainable industry. We are honouring and working with, not taking away from, our Aboriginal brothers and sisters.

We want to show you how to create truly Australian food at home – without labelling it as only 'bush tucker' or thinking you have to forage for hours in the bush. With a few small adjustments and a little experimentation with what we normally use in the kitchen, we can all eat delicious food that is better for the Australian environment, better for our cultural understanding of our nation's first people, is more sustainable and celebrates the amazing-tasting food that is truly local.

As the oldest living culture on the earth, Indigenous Australians were the first to harvest, process, prepare and consume the vast array of native plant species. Finally now in 2019 we can see an industry that is no longer a novelty (to some) and finally being championed for the powerful, ancient, healthy taste sensation that it is. These plants we refer to in the book are not just about food. They are an untapped medicinal, cosmetic, nutraceutical and pharmaceutical world we have only just scraped the surface of. And when I say we, I mean anyone non-Indigenous. We will, very sadly, never know how much traditional knowledge has been lost since European settlers dispossessed Indigenous family groups of their traditional lands, stories, family, language, culture and foods. More often than not, Aboriginal people were forced (often violently) to stop anything traditional to them.

They were forced to replace their way of hunting, gathering and farming food with a way that did not suit our Australian climate. In turn, our soil has been degraded, species – both animal and plant – have been lost, and a race that was as healthy as it gets is now living with chronic disease brought on by unnatural food and a completely opposite way of living.

This always gets me thinking. When you try many of these ingredients for the first time, they are radically different to what our palate is used to. Bitter, astringent, sour. So often, when people try these native foods they pull faces worthy of a meme and it sometimes takes a few times to enjoy it. That in itself makes me realise that we need to eat for nutrients (not just taste). We need to see food as medicine. As purpose. Our Indigenous peoples eat seasonally. Some groups have up to twelve seasons per year. Each season has purpose. Eating Kakadu plum when in season, with its extremely high vitamin C content, would be nature's flu jab.

Australia once contained a glorious bounty of wild edible plant species that ran into the thousands (so many have been lost), ranging from starchy seeds and sour fruits to tubers, leaves, seaweeds and proteins. Today, knowing how to identify edible plants is not easy. The incredibly knowledgeable Aboriginal people know about which plants are edible, which plants are poisonous, and which plants are poisonous but can be prepared in certain ways that make them safe to eat – information that would have been acquired over generations (60,000 years) of trial and error. Plant foods supplied up to 80 per cent of their diet in desert regions, and as little as 40 per cent in coastal areas, where shellfish, fish and game were abundant. Diets and food preparation techniques varied from one region to another and also from one group to another. It was not a one-size-fits-all diet, like it feels in today's modern life when you enter a supermarket.

So let's instead make use of nature's supermarket. Our own backyard. Our truly local food. Let's use food as an opportunity to connect with our nation's first people, to reconcile, to respect a deep and long culture. We all eat, three times a day. If we all want it, we can create demand for native food, give our Indigenous communities opportunity and respect, and give our farmers a value-added proposition rich in culture and rich in repairing our soil. Our people need this, our environment needs this and most of all our bodies need this. Eat local. *Like, properly.*

We hope this book will be the beginning of a magical journey for you. That it will encourage you to ask questions, to learn about our rich Indigenous culture, try some new things, experiment in your kitchen, be patient and help this wonderful industry grow by supporting it where you can: start by replacing limes with finger limes or black pepper with native pepper and, most importantly, become more connected to our incredible land and its first people, just like we did.

Gratitude, love & lemon myrtle,
Rebecca

Ingredients

In the pages following, we list our favourite ingredients and how we like to use them. If you can't get the native ingredients listed in a recipe because of seasonality or supply, there is always an equivalent. For example, instead of wild basil use English basil, for sea rosemary use rosemary, or for river mint use peppermint. Try the frozen or dried version of the native ingredient if you can't get it fresh. Please don't let it put you off trying the recipe if you can't get it the first time you try. Have a read of the ingredients table on pages 244–247. Most importantly, enjoy experimenting, just like we do.

Anise myrtle *(Syzygium anisatum)*

This rainforest species has leaves with strong liquorice and aniseed flavours. Also known as aniseed myrtle and ringwood, it is found naturally in the subtropical rainforests of northern New South Wales. Anise myrtle leaf is one of the highest sources of the compound anethole, which gives it the aniseed flavour and aroma, and you will see why when you use it at home.

Banksia *(Banksia spp.)*

Orange and yellow banksias grow all over our continent. Not just for decorating your house or garden, these flowers also make a beautiful nectar drink when soaked in water. Traditionally, the flowers were sucked for a little sweet hit. They must be picked and used when filled with nectar, always leaving many behind for regeneration and the wildlife, of course. You can use the flowers of silver banksias and swamp banksias for this, too.

Barilla spinach *(Tetragonia implexicoma)*

Also called bower spinach, with yellow flowers and bright-red berries (used for dye), this spinach is a beauty. It is high in antioxidants, like warrigal greens. Use it like English spinach, best blanched first.

Blood lime *(Citrus australasica)*

A hybrid fruit cross between a finger lime and mandarin; fabulous and a wonderful addition to your cooking. Grill in halves on the barbecue and use as a garnish.

Bloodroot *(Haemodorum spicatum)*

Like a curry that keeps on giving. This striking red root (which looks a lot like a fennel bulb) is absolutely amazing. Anything you cook with it will take on its colour. Use sparingly, as it genuinely packs a punch. This bulb vegetable has long been used by the Noongar Aboriginal people of Western Australia both as a food source and as medicine.

Boab *(Adansonia gregorii)*

An iconic tree throughout the Northern Territory. Boabs produce large fruits around 10 cm in diameter. The inside has a chalky nut that tastes a little like sherbet and is amazing crushed and sprinkled on food. Excellent fresh but can also be frozen.

Boobialla or Native juniper *(Myoporum insulare)*

This salt-tolerant shrub is also known as common or coastal boobialla and produces sweet astringent berries. Not really one for eating fresh off the bush, unless you love a mouth pucker, the aromatic, juniper-like berries work well in jams and preserves.

Boonjie tamarind *(Diploglottis bracteata)*

This bright-red, stunning-looking, tasty, tangy fruit is a refreshing treat eaten raw or it can be cooked creatively in many ways (especially great as a paste, chutney and sauce). With very few trees left remaining in the wild of northern New South Wales, this endangered species is worth using to try and protect it. Create a demand! Our favourite place to get these babies from is Rainforest Bounty in the Atherton Tablelands.

Bunya pine (Araucaria bidwillii)

Think dinosaurs. Apparently they ate these nuts too. These gigantic trees produce pine cones so big that in falling they can actually kill people by falling on their heads. The cones have many kernels inside which need cracking prior to eating. They are best fresh but can also be frozen. The bunya nut is high in protein, carbohydrates and good fat. The flavour reminds me of a pine nut, and the bunya can be used in the same way.

Bush/Lady/White apple (Syzygium forte)

These golf ball–sized apples come in beautiful scarlet colours. The fruit has a large seed, but the flesh is soft and tart. We love them fresh, sliced in salads or just eaten like an apple (but navigating the seed). They can also be frozen whole for later use or dehydrated.

Bush tomato, kutjera or desert raisin (Solanum centrale)

Oh so wonderful when eaten fresh but the flavour profile of a dried one is also amazing, like a caramel, savoury carob crossed with sun-dried tomato. The fruits can actually be left to dry on the bush and collected months later. They are best ground, and can be used in just about any dish you like. Bush tomato has superior antioxidant capacity compared to the blueberry, which is renowned worldwide as a health-promoting fruit.

Chocolate lily (Arthropodium strictum) and Vanilla lily (Arthropodium milleflorum)

Pretty little purple and white flowers mainly found in Victoria and New South Wales but rather excitingly we have them growing on our farm in South Australia. The tiny white and purple flowers have a strong caramel and chocolate perfume in the springtime. They have edible roots, too.

Cinnamon myrtle (Backhousia myrtifolia)

This lovely rainforest tree has cream flowers and cinnamon-scented leaves. While you will probably buy it in dried leaf form, all you need to do is grind it in a spice grinder and keep it in a little airtight jar. Use it in place of traditional cinnamon wherever you can, though use a little less as it's much stronger in flavour.

Davidson's plum (Davidsonia jerseyana)

Found growing in the rainforests in Queensland and northern New South Wales, these trees are tall and slender and the leaves and fruit have irritant hairs. The fruit are bright purple with an almost magenta flesh. These plums are super-tart but make wonderful sauces, jams and ferments.

Desert lime (Citrus glauca)

Like the sherbet bomb you ate as a kid! These limes are so tangy and delicious, we use them at home in everything. We have a huge container of them in the freezer and pop them into gin and tonics, cakes, stir-fries, salads – just about anything that wants a fresh lime addition. The best part is they freeze whole and can be eaten whole too. They are also a very rich source of calcium and contain high levels of vitamin C, folate (vitamin B9), vitamin E and lutein.

Anise myrtle

Blood lime

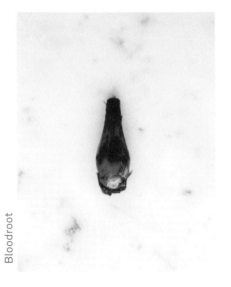

Bloodroot

Boobialla

Boonjie tamarind

Bottlebrush

Bunya nut

Bush apple

Bush tomato/kutjera

Chocolate lily

Cinnamon myrtle

Davidson's plum

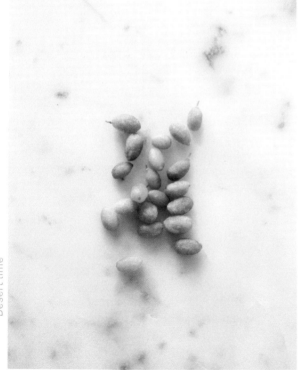

Desert lime

Finger lime

Finger lime (Citrus australasica)

Endemic to south-east Queensland and northern New South Wales, the finger lime tree has fruit in a range of vibrant colours, from green through to red. The fruit is rich in folate, potassium and vitamin E, as well as the more usual citrus benefits such as vitamin C. While the flavour can be compared to a lime, the fruit has tiny 'caviar pearls' of flesh prized by chefs worldwide. It is used in a variety of ways, from topping ceviche and oysters, to salads and cocktails. Our personal favourite is finger lime over kangaroo carpaccio.

Fish rushes (Ficinia nodosa)

These are used in cooking by the Ngarrindjeri people for cooking their local fish, the Coorong mullet. Use them for smoking fish and meat.

Geraldton wax (Chamelaucium uncinatum)

Another of our favourites. The leaves of this shrub have the most wonderful aroma and taste like a lemony pine needle. They are delicious in anything with seafood and especially stuffed in whole fish. The flowers are also edible, but not in large quantities.

Green ants (Oecophylla smaragdina)

These beauties are incredible and we buy them from the Larrakia people, who harvest them ethically. These ants taste like citrus crossed with coriander seed and are an amazing and exciting garnish.

Illawarra plum (Podocarpus elatus)

Deep purple and small in size, these plums are also known as daalgal, goongum and pine plums. The flesh is connected to a rather large inedible seed so they are a little bit of work but worth it by way of a sweet and piney-flavoured flesh reward. This tree is found growing in rainforests on the east coast of Australia.

Island celery (Apium insulare)

From Flinders Island and Bass Strait, this plant looks like celery and has a really strong celery flavour so just sub old-school celery out and island celery in for the win. No big stalks but flavourful leaves.

Kakadu plum (Terminalia ferdinandiana)

We have not had a cold or flu for years because we take the plum (known as gubinge among many other names) in powder form in a shot of water when travelling or feeling run-down. It is known for being one of the highest sources of vitamin C on the planet and is honestly the one bush medicine I urge you all to get on to. It can be eaten raw and is about the size of an olive and pale green in colour. It also has a large seed like an olive.

Karkalla or Pig face (Carpobrotus rossii)

More succulent than anything else, imagine a juicy, crunchy and salty green. It is delicious. The flowers are edible too and when it fruits, expect salty little fig-like berries in a stunning shade of pink. You will never walk past it again without stopping for a nibble. The plant grows low to the ground, mainly on the coast, but it is super-resilient and can be grown from cuttings. Add to salads, stir-fries, pickle it, ferment it, and eat it!

Lemon aspen (Acronychia acidula)

This is a type of citrus bearing small edible fruits that taste like a cross between a lime and a grapefruit with a hint of conifer. It is a rich source of folate, iron and zinc, and also contains magnesium and calcium. Because the lemon aspen is a rainforest species, the fruit may sometimes be referred to as 'rainforest lemon'. This tree is native to Far North Queensland, but will grow as far south as Sydney and even in South Australia.

Lemon myrtle (Backhousia citriodora)

I suspect all of you would have at least heard of this beauty. The lemon myrtle is a rainforest tree in the family of Myrtaceae. Not just a perfect cooking addition, the leaves are also the purest source of natural citral (90–98%), making lemon myrtle a powerful essential oil, thus a powerful medicine. It has a refreshing, clean citrus aroma and taste, and goes in just about everything. Dubbed the 'Queen of Herbs' she is more lemony than a lemon will ever be.

Lemon-scented gum (Corymbia citriodora)

Much like lemon myrtle, these leaves are high in citronella and pack a lemony punch. We have a bunch hanging upside down that helps keep the mozzies away and keeps the house smelling divine, and use it in teas and in cooking, just ripping a few leaves off as needed. I love to add five leaves to my batches of bone broth.

Lilly pilly (Syzygium spp.)

There are many varieties of lilly pilly with fruits in shades varying from vibrant magenta to cherry red and blue. Australia has dozens of species. The tart little fruit has hints of clove and Granny Smith apple and when eaten fresh are like a tiny burst of apple pie filling (before the sugar is added, of course). Eat them fresh, cooked, pickled or preserved. They can also be stored in the freezer, but will lose their colour when thawed or cooked (sadly, because the colour is stunning). Aside from fresh in salads and desserts, I love them pickled so that I can use them for months post their short season. They do have tiny seeds in them but these are edible and give some texture.

Macadamia (Macadamia integrifolia)

The magic nut. Both tasty and healthy. Have you ever tried to crack one, though? Bloody hard. That is why they are expensive. But they are totally worth it. Macadamias are great in savoury and sweet dishes, and make amazing nut milk (like, the best). The trees are only native to Australia (even though Hawaii and South Africa sell as much as we do).

Mayaka/Bush pear (Marsdenia australis)

Such an important food plant to the Adnyamathanha people. Young leaves and nectar-rich flowers as well as the beautiful pods. These are a little like sprout cucumbers with a hint of sweet inside. They're great raw or cooked on a fire.

Minra/Bullock bush (Alectryon oleifolius)

Found in the Flinders Ranges, the fruit of this bush is bright orange with a large seed pod in the centre. It reminds us of a chocolate orange and can be eaten fresh or dried.

Muntries or Native apple (Kunzea pomifera)

These little beauties are found on low-growing shrubs that are native to the south coast of Australia. Also called emu apple or native cranberry, they are known for their antioxidant value, which is around four times higher than that of blueberries. With a spicy apple flavour and a pretty red and green tinge, your kids will think they have won the fairy lottery in apples and eat them like candy. Much like they used to be traditionally, they can be used dried or pounded and made into a paste and dried into a strap. I love them fresh in salads.

Murnong or Yam daisy (Microseris lanceolata)

I squealed so loud when my yam daisies produced pretty yellow flowers then delicious

Geraldton wax

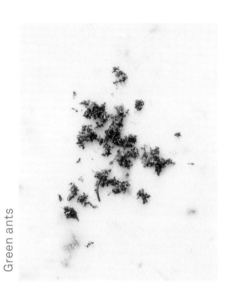

Green ants

Fish rushes

Ingredients

Illawarra plum

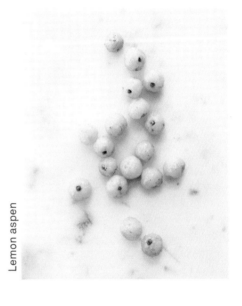

Lemon aspen

Kakadu plum

Karkalla

Lilly pilly

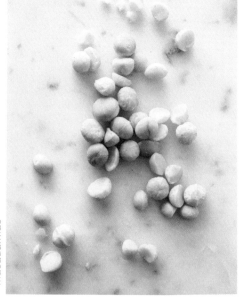

Macadamias

Mayaka/Bush pear

Ingredients

Minra/Bullock bush

Muntries

Native currant

little roots! These are hugely important to the Wurundjeri people as a vital carbohydrate source. The introduction of sheep, however, rendered the plants almost extinct. A lot of work is going on to make them abundant again. I do hope you all get to try them and one day buy them like you would potatoes.

Native cherry or Cherry Ballart (Exocarpos cupressiformis)

These are amazing tiny astringent pops of tartness, so not really like the cherries you would be used to. Plus, they take a lot of time and effort to harvest by hand.

Native currant (Acrotriche depressa)

These are very rare in the wild but grown sustainably by Outback Pride. The currants have an incredible colour and are wonderful in drinks.

Native curry bush (Cassinia laevis)

We first discovered this while we were out foraging with Damien's uncle, Noel. It looks like a pretty unassuming, low shrubby bush but when you pick the leaves, the waft of curry powder is everywhere. It's quite amazing. The curry bush was said to be used medicinally for toothaches and tummy aches. Use it ground, just like curry powder.

Native lemongrass (Cymbopogon ambiguus)

Not as juicy as the lemongrass you might be used to. The stalks are sturdy grass with fluffy tops and are a very pale straw-like colour. Aside from being excellent bush medicine in the treatment of things like colds and headaches, it has a beautiful lemon sherbet flavour. We use it in our three-lemon tea but it can be used in broths, to stuff meat or infused into all kinds of sweet treats like the chocolate truffle recipe on page 198.

Native orange (Capparis mitchellii)

Stunning flowers and gorgeous fruit too. It has many seeds like a passionfruit and ripens in summer. It is very high in vitamin C.

Native raspberry (Rubus probus)

Native raspberry is a slightly paler red than an English raspberry and has a tarter taste and softer flesh. It has a very short season and shelf life so is best eaten fresh but can be frozen too.

Native thyme (Prostanthera incisa)

This is definitely our favourite of the local herbs and we use it in our Native Thyme Oil. Sometimes called cut-leaf mint (you'll know why when the menthol aroma hits), this herb was used by Indigenous Australians for its medicinal properties but we now use it in cooking. Best fresh but also potent dried and ground. Very easy to grow at home directly in the ground or in small pots on a balcony if you have a smaller space.

Ooray plum (Davidsonia pruriens)

These grow from the far tropical north of Australia to northern New South Wales. With 100 times the vitamin C of oranges, they are seriously jam-packed with all of the good things. Sadly, the fruiting season is super-short (December to January) so you will more often than not buy them frozen, which is perfectly fine; just thaw them out on paper towel. They are often referred to as 'sour plum' and you will know why the first time you bite into one; they are highly acidic. Most people make them into jams and chutneys but I like the acidity so choose to use them sliced ever so thinly in salads, stew them for side dishes with meats or use them in casseroles. My favourite in summer is to cook them with Illawarra plums and Victoria plums and use them in a trifle.

Pandanus (Pandanus spp.)

Probably up there with the most glorious looking plants, spiky leaved and almost pineapple-like, the pandanus is of very important use to Aboriginal people. The nuts or kernels can be eaten raw or cooked, as well as the new leaves (the soft white part). The leaves also make incredible baskets and are used for weaving. This nut is considered a luxury and we couldn't agree more. Try it fermented, pickled, toasted or raw.

Parakeelya (Calandrinia balonensis)

An absolutely stunning edible flower. It grows in the desert and both the flowers and seed heads are used by the Pitjantjatjara people.

Pepperberry (Tasmannia lanceolata syn. Drimys lanceolata)

Also known as mountain pepper leaf and mountain pepper, these aromatic shrubs grow naturally in the forest and the cool climate of southern New South Wales, Victoria and Tasmania. Traditionally, the plant was used for its incredible antiseptic properties as well as its flavour. Both the leaves and fruit are used. Aboriginal people suffering from sore gums and toothaches would crush the berries with water to make a paste and applied the paste to treat the infection. Chewing on the berries gives you a little antioxidant boost too. Wherever we use pepper in the book, use dried berries unless leaf is stated and I urge you to fill your pepper grinder with this instead of regular pepper.

Quandong or urti (Santalum acuminatum)

Also known as the native peach, the quandong is probably one of the more common Indigenous ingredients in our pantry today and it also happens to be an icon in the Flinders Ranges where Damien is from. It comes in many shades of pink right through to jewel-like red. It's a popular fruit for its tartness but is also widely prized for the large seed/kernel inside, which is used to make jewellery. It's high in vitamin C.

Rainforest cherry (Syzygium aqueum)

Found in the rainforests of New South Wales, this tree has stunning bright-red fruit. We love this cherry in everything from salads to desserts. It's tart with a hint of sweetness. If you can't get it fresh, use frozen and thawed.

Riberry (Syzygium luehmannii)

This tiny bright-pink berry is sweet and sour, spicy and almost clove-like. So mighty, it is said to be ace at preventing or delaying diseases such as Alzheimer's, autoimmune and cardiovascular diseases, cancer and diabetes. Riberry also has high levels of folate, otherwise known as vitamin B12.

River mint (Mentha australis)

Another one for the plant pot. I would highly recommend using this in place of any call for mint. It is a cross between peppermint and spearmint in flavour and is also a wonderful medicinal herb. Use it fresh when possible but it is also great and very pungent when dried.

Rosella (Hibiscus sabdariffa)

Whilst not exclusively native to Australia, our rosella has developed a personality to make it our own. It has stunning red flowers that produce a sweet and tart flavour that goes well in just about anything. They are also really high in vitamin C.

Saltbush (Atriplex spp.)

If you tell any farmers over the age of 60 that saltbush is now a bit of a delicacy, they

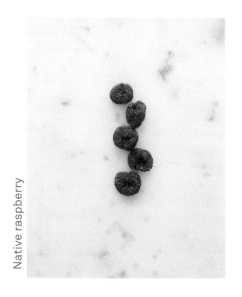

Native raspberry

Native thyme

Parakeelya

Pandanus

Pepperberry

Rainforest cherry

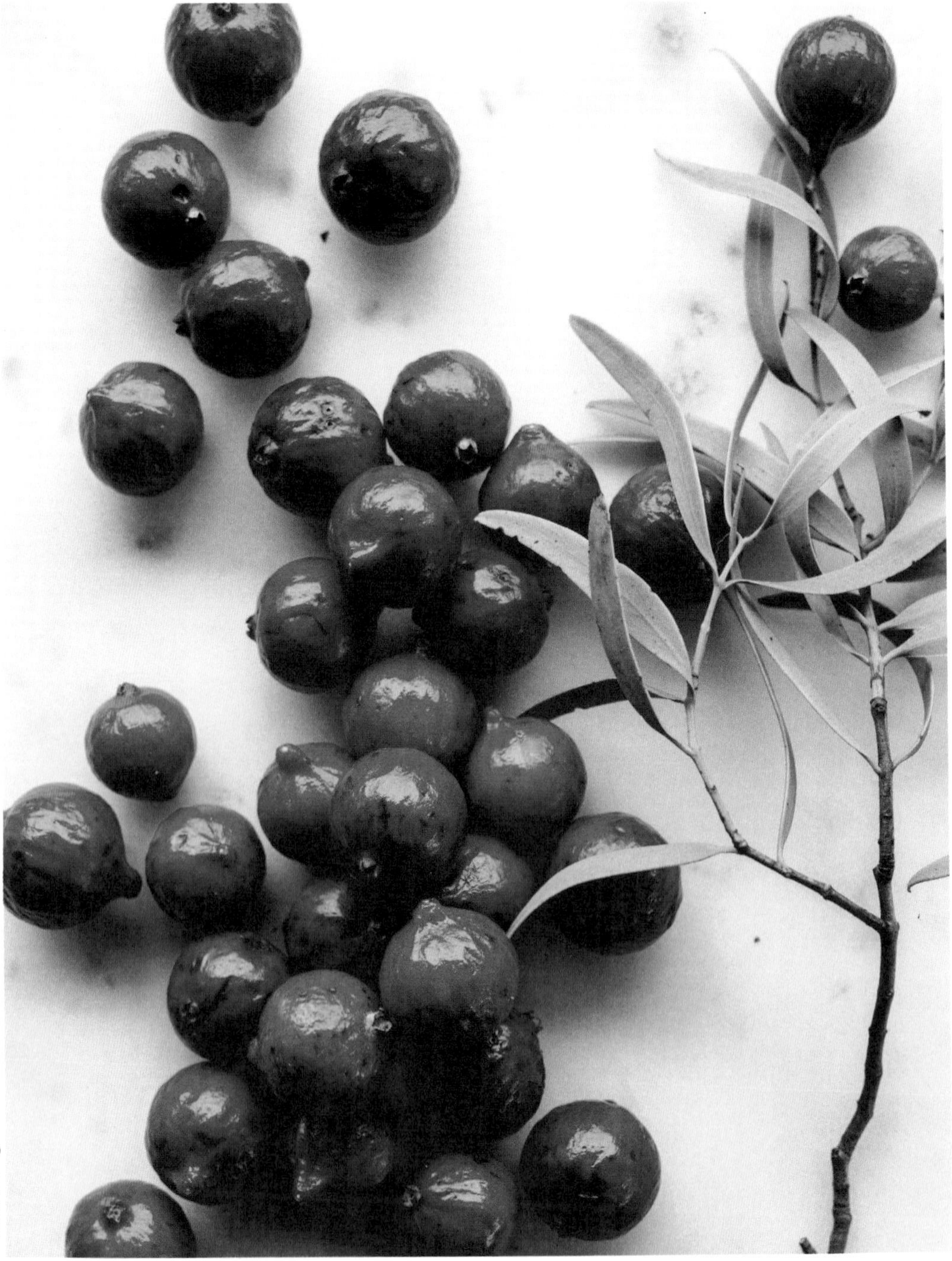

Quandong/urti

Riberry

Rosella

River mint

Saltbush

Sandalwood

Sea parsley

Samphire

Sunrise lime

Seablite

Sea rosemary

would laugh in your face. A bit like the lamb shank, which was once fed to the farm dogs but is now one of the priciest cuts in the butcher's shop, saltbush was only eaten by the sheep. Alas, it should be eaten by us all – it is wonderful. A huge number of seeds come from the flowering after spring and autumn and they are like little salty popcorn kernels, but were also ground and mixed with water to make dough cooked in coals. We have loads on our farm, as I walk around I just pick it and nibble on it. A bit like the sheep. Note: there are many different species of saltbush. We tend to use old man saltbush the most.

Samphire (Tecticornia spp.)

A genus of salt-tolerant, ground-hugging succulents, some of which are endemic or unique to Australia. The genus contains several species, many of which are edible and are commonly referred to as sea asparagus, swamp grass, salicorn, glasswort, pickleweed and sea beans. Best blanched like asparagus; serve with roast lamb, in stir-fries and salads.

Sandalwood nut (Santalum spicatum)

Best known for its oil, these nuts are a fabulous eating nut too. They remind us of rice puff cereal and are great seasoned and toasted.

Seablite (Suaeda australis)

This plant can be found growing wild around much of South Australia's coastline and estuarine salt marshes. The leaves will impart a pleasant, salty flavour to a dish and in small quantities make a nice addition to a salad. Seablite can be cooked with other vegetables to enhance flavour and add a natural saltiness.

Sea parsley (Apium prostratum)

We like to think of these as mini celery plants. They look like celery and taste a bit like it too. Treat them like a herb or vegetable. Although sea parsley is a close relative to the European version of parsley, it packs a more peppery punch and has much more flavour and health benefits too. In fact it was used by early Australian settlers in the prevention of scurvy.

Sea rosemary (Olearia axillaris)

A silvery version of the rosemary you would be used to seeing, sea rosemary grows so easily and loves coastal soils. It is way tastier than your everyday rosemary and has the most delectable aroma too. Use it whenever you would use rosemary. This was one of the first native plants to be used by Europeans.

Strawberry gum (Eucalyptus olida)

A medium-size tree which grows in the Northern Tablelands of New South Wales, this beauty has many health benefits, including antioxidant, antifungal and antibiotic properties. It has also been shown to help balance microflora of the gut. The leaves have a strawberry and cream aroma and show up beautifully in an array of cooking styles. We love them best in tea and sweets (especially the pavlova on page 211).

Sunrise lime (Citrus australasica)

Shaped like a small pear, with a tangy cumquat flavour, these limes are a stunning yellow colour and perfect in just about everything.

Warrigal greens (Tetragonia tetragonioides)

Also known as native spinach, New Zealand spinach or Botany Bay greens, this is one of the most common edible native plants. The leaves must be blanched before eating, as they contain oxalates which in high quantities can have adverse effects. I'm not going to lie, I do munch on them raw (just not too many). Simply blanch in boiling water for about 10–15 seconds, remove and refresh under cold water. They are naturally very high in antioxidants and as good for you as spinach.

Wattleseed (Acacia victoriae)

Acacia seeds are very important foods to Aboriginal people; they are extremely nutritious, yielding protein levels of 18–25 per cent, and sometimes high levels of fat, too. The nectar forms sugar-like crystals on the trunks and branches of many kinds of wattles. Only some of the many hundreds of wattle species produce seed that is commercially or wild harvested today for consumption, and it must be roasted before eating or the seeds will break your teeth. With the flavour of toasted coffee beans, sweet spice, raisin and chocolate, these seeds are deservedly popular today.Try a variety of different species.

Wild basil (Ocimum tenuiflorum)

Ah, the wild basil. Related to Asian holy basil, this beauty packs a punch. This is an annual plant with pretty purple flowers. It is believed to have been naturalised to withstand the harsh Australian climate hundreds of years ago by Indonesian traders pre-European settlement. Use it, in smaller quantities, wherever you would use European basil.

Youlk (Platysace deflexa)

The roots of this plant look like a potato and taste like a nashi pear and a radish crossed with kohlrabi and potato. It stays crunchy even after cooking, with an awesome juicy flavour. Native to south-west Australia where it grows in the sandy soil, it is an important food for the Noongar people, even if its availability was quite compromised by massive deforestation following European settlement. One single plant produces several roots, but only a few can be harvested at a time, allowing the plant to regenerate. Commercialisation of this veggie is well underway. We hope one day it will sit proudly next to the potato.

Strawberry gum

Ingredients

Warrigal greens

Wild basil

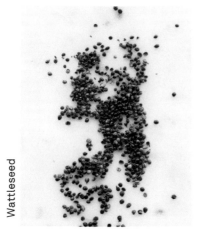

Wattleseed

Youlk

Nuts, Seeds & Roots

Macadamias are the best-known native nut, but our country offers many more varieties for us to enjoy. Sadly, not all are commercially available yet but sandalwood, bunya (my personal favourite), pandanus and boab are and most certainly worth a try. Nut trees are found all over Australia but the majority of them grow in forests and rainforests. In Queensland alone there are about ten different nuts found locally.

In the Central Desert, seeds of native grasses, shrubs, herbs and trees still form a very important part of Aboriginal people's diet. It is said that dozens of seed species were eaten in this area. All over the country, edible seeds of acacias and grasses have been used by many different Aboriginal groups for tens of thousands of years. Some were eaten raw but others had to be processed or prepared before eating, and grinding seed is also an ancient survival skill.

Acacias, in particular, provide a range of traditional foods; from their seeds to their sweet nectar (nori or 'bush lolly' as Damien's family call it). Seed from about 50 acacia species are used in the industry today, although some, such as *Acacia victoriae* (gundabluey), were and still are preferable to others. The high nutritional value and wide availability of seed from various species make them a valuable resource in arid areas. Like all of the native ingredients in this book, seeds serve a purpose in the grand scheme of seasons, cycles and culture. We have found that the easiest way for most of us to start integrating these amazing ingredients into our everyday cooking is to use the spices – the ground seeds and roots. Some of these ingredients can be a little harder to get (we're hoping that will change in the very near future). Use what you can get, and spices are definitely the easiest to get your hands on. Unlike traditional and time-consuming ways of gathering and preparing these ingredients, today all it takes is a quick search on the internet to find places to buy them from and in these pages you'll find easy ways to make them part of your everyday cooking.

Bushfood Brittle

The perfect sweet and sour candy. Sweet from the brittle and sour from the tangy limes. A great gift for every occasion, too.

Makes 1 sheet

Prep Time: 5 minutes
Cooking Time: 10 minutes

1½ cups caster or raw sugar
¼ cup freeze-dried finger lime
¼ cup dried rose petals
¼ cup sandalwood nuts

Preheat oven to 220°C.

Place the sugar in an even layer on a large baking tray lined with baking paper. Cook for 10–15 minutes, turning tray halfway until sugar has melted and is caramelised. (It will start to melt from the edges in.)

Spread with a palette knife if there are any patches of sugar that have not started to melt.

Remove from the oven and sprinkle with freeze-dried finger limes, rose petals and sandalwood nuts. Set aside for 10 minutes to set.

Break into shards to serve. This brittle can be stored in an airtight container for up to a week.

Warndu Dukkah

This recipe was developed by a very special person to Warndu, Taylor. She worked with us for a couple of years. This is her recipe and we bloody love it. It's close to being all native ingredients too (except the sesame seeds)!

Serves 10

Prep Time: 3 minutes
Cooking Time: 5 minutes

200 g macadamias
100 g sesame seeds
15 g wattleseed, roasted not ground
3 g native thyme, dried and ground
3 g lemon myrtle, dried and ground
1 g wild basil, dried and ground
3 g pepperberries, crushed
5 g Murray River pink salt
25 g bush tomato, dried and ground

Preheat the oven to 220°C.

On a baking tray, spread out the macadamias and toast for a few minutes, or until golden brown. Remove and let cool. Blitz in a food processor for a few seconds, or until you get small crumb.

Lightly toast the sesame seeds on the same tray used for the macadamias for a minute. Remove and cool.

In a large bowl, mix all the ingredients together and then transfer to an airtight container. This dukkah will last a few weeks but make sure no moisture gets in, as macadamias are oily and will go rancid if not stored properly. Best made in small batches.

Macadamia Milk

This recipe makes a creamy, absolutely delicious dairy-free milk.
It froths perfectly for an amazing flat white! Make small batches
frequently for better shelf life. You can add more honey if you want
a sweeter milk.

Makes 1 litre

Prep Time: 5 minutes

800 ml filtered water
160 g raw macadamias
pinch of salt
1 teaspoon raw honey

Note: *Keep the leftover ground
nuts from the milk and dry out for
macadamia meal (and make our pie
crust recipe on page 50!)*

Place all the ingredients into a blender and blitz for no
more than 30 seconds.

Pour through a sieve. Store in a clean bottle and use
within 4–5 days. Always shake the bottle before use.
(It has a very different scent to most nut milks, so don't
be put off.)

Macadamia Pie Crust

We use this pie crust for just about anything that needs a pastry base, both sweet and savoury, from quiches to fruit pies. It makes an amazing pumpkin or potato pie. It's also great for a fruit crumble: just make another half quantity of the recipe and sprinkle it over the top after you've filled the crust with fruit.

Serves 8

Prep Time: 5 minutes
Cooking Time: 10 minutes

coconut oil, for greasing
2 tablespoons macadamia oil
2½ cups macadamia meal
2 tablespoons buckwheat flour
1 free-range egg

Note: Keep in an airtight container for up to 3 days. This pie crust can be made with other nuts and nut oils.

Preheat the oven to 175°C. Grease a small pie dish (about 20 cm or smaller for a thicker crust) with coconut oil. If you have one, use a springform or detachable dish.

In a small bowl, mix all the remaining ingredients together. Push evenly into the pie dish or tin, across the bottom and up the sides.

Bake for 10–12 minutes. Oil will froth from the pie crust but there is no need to worry, it will subside once cool. You can also blot with paper towel after you remove the crust from the oven. Set aside until ready to use.

Strawberry Gum Macaroons

This version of the classic macaroon (not macaron!) uses our beautiful macadamia nut. It is also gluten-free. Try cinnamon, lemon or anise myrtle alternatives, too.

Makes 10

Prep Time: 5 minutes
Cooking Time: 30 minutes

3 free-range egg whites
110 g macadamias
22 g sugar
2 tablespoons rice flour
2 tablespoons coconut flour
¼ cup shredded coconut
1 teaspoon ground strawberry gum
10 macadamias, halved for decoration

Preheat the oven to 180°C. Line a baking tray with baking paper.

In a large bowl, whisk the egg whites until frothy. Set aside.

Blitz the macadamias in a food processor for a few seconds until they form a paste. Transfer to the bowl containing the egg and add the remaining ingredients except the macadamia halves. Mix until just combined, don't overmix.

Scoop tablespoons of the mixture onto the tray, leaving a few centimetres between each biscuit. Top each one with a macadamia half. Bake for 20–30 minutes, or until golden brown. If you like a chewy inside, bake for less time.

Damien's Damper

An all-round show-stopper, this one. Impress your mates with your bread-making skills, with little skill at all! Try playing around with any bush spice until you find your favourite. This is best cooked in a fire but an oven will do just as well.

Serves 6

Prep Time: 15 minutes
Cooking Time: 15 minutes

2 tablespoons macadamia or lemon myrtle infused oil
300–350 ml water
500 g self-raising flour, plus extra for dusting
pinch of salt
2 tablespoons roasted and ground wattleseed (or lemon myrtle, straw-berry gum, bush tomato or saltbush)

If using the oven, preheat to 220°C.

Mix the oil and water in a jug. Sift the flour into a large bowl, and mix through the salt and wattleseed. Slowly pour in the oil and water, and mix to make a dough.

Turn out the dough onto a floured surface and knead until smooth. Dust with flour, place on a baking tray and bake in the oven for 15–20 minutes, or ideally wrap in foil and cook on a fire in the ashes. Damper is always best eaten hot with lashings of butter.

Wattleseed Coffee

The most perfect caffeine-free coffee alternative. You still get
a little kick and the same nutty, chocolatey profile and mouthfeel
as coffee, but without the crash!

Serves 1

Prep Time: 2 minutes

1–2 teaspoons roasted and ground
  wattleseed
1 cup boiling water
macadamia milk, to taste (see recipe
  page 49)
honey, to taste (optional)

Place the wattleseed in a coffee plunger or cafetière.

Boil the water and pour into the plunger. Leave to brew
for 3 minutes, plunge and pour into a mug. Add a dash of
macadamia milk, some honey if you like, and drink.

Wattleseed, Macadamia & Lemon Myrtle Bliss Balls

This recipe is a total no-brainer. All of these amazing native spices just go perfectly in a bliss ball, but I would highly recommend playing around with this recipe and using your favourite combinations.

Makes 20

Prep Time: 5 minutes
Fridge Time: 1 hour

1 cup pitted prunes
1½ cups quinoa, cooked and cooled
4 tablespoons macadamia or
  almond meal
3 tablespoons sunflower seeds
3 tablespoons raw cacao powder
4 tablespoons maple syrup
½ cup kefir (optional)
1 teaspoon ground cinnamon myrtle
2 tablespoons macadamia butter
1 teaspoon lemon myrtle powder
2 tablespoons chia seeds
1 tablespoon wattleseed extract or
  roasted ground wattleseed
pinch of Murray River pink salt
pinch of anise myrtle powder
1 tablespoon macadamia oil
shredded coconut, crushed nuts or
  roasted ground wattleseed, for coating

Blitz the prunes in a food processor. Place the prunes in a large bowl with all the ingredients except shredded coconut, and mix together.

Roll the mixture into balls and then roll the balls in the coconut to coat. Store in an airtight container in the fridge. They will keep for about 2 weeks.

Wattleseed, Carob & Macadamia Brownies

Who doesn't love a brownie?! I have never, ever met such a person.
This brownie has a fairly unique taste and if you don't like carob,
simply leave it out.

Makes 8

Prep Time: 10 minutes
Cooking Time: 25 minutes

65 g butter
250 g sugar
2 free-range egg whites
3 tablespoons raw cacao powder
125 g self-raising flour
½ tablespoon carob syrup or honey
1 tablespoon roasted ground
   wattleseed
100 g toasted macadamias, chopped
3 tablespoons macadamia oil
pinch of salt

For the icing:
125 g butter, at room temperature
70 g icing sugar
120 g dark chocolate, melted
1 teaspoon roasted ground wattleseed
roasted whole wattleseed, for sprinkling
edible flowers, for garnish

Preheat the oven to 180°C. Line a loaf, lamington or similar tin with baking paper so you can pull the brownie out when cooked.

Place the butter and sugar into the bowl of a stand mixer and begin to cream together on a low speed. Add the egg whites while still beating on low, then add the cacao powder and flour a little at a time. Add the carob syrup, wattleseed, macadamias, macadamia oil and salt. Beat on a medium speed until all mixed together. Don't overmix, it really just needs to be combined.

Pour the mixture into the lined tray and bake for 25 minutes. I like my brownie soft and chewy, so this timing is perfect. The syrup helps to create a chewy corner on the brownie. You can bake it for a few minutes longer if you like it firmer. Allow to cool.

To make the icing: Beat the butter and icing sugar in a medium bowl with a hand mixer until pale and fluffy. Mix the wattleseed into the melted chocolate and slowly add to the icing. Stir through. Ice the brownies and sprinkle with roasted whole wattleseed, if using, and garnish with flowers.

Spiced Eggnog

Delicious, boozy and worth the hangover! And not just for Christmas Day! Don't taste it too frequently as it's quite strong! You can leave the booze out for a spiced milk, and it's also lovely hot in winter.

Serves 10

Prep Time: 30 minutes
Fridge Time: 2 hours

6 free-range eggs
1 cup sugar
½ teaspoon vanilla extract
1 tablespoon orange or rose blossom
 water
1 teaspoon ground strawberry gum
1 teaspoon wattleseed, extract or
 ground
1 teaspoon grated nutmeg
½ teaspoon ground cinnamon myrtle
½ teaspoon ground anise myrtle
4 cardamom pods, crushed
180 ml brandy
80 ml dark rum (we use Bundaberg)
500 ml full-cream milk
500 ml thick cream
crushed ice, to serve
edible flowers, ground cinnamon myrtle
 and grated nutmeg, for garnish

Note: Any sugar will do, but I like dark brown sugar, as it has a more distinct taste.

Chill all the ingredients first.

In a large bowl, beat the eggs until they are frothy, then beat in the sugar, vanilla, blossom water and all the spices. Stir in the brandy, then the rum. Slowly stir in the milk, then the cream.

Strain and serve over crushed ice (it is Christmas in Australia, after all) with flowers, cinnamon myrtle and grated nutmeg sprinkled on top.

Nuts, Seeds & Roots

Christmas Cake

You can make these in smaller tins for the most wonderful Christmas gift for family and friends. If you have time, make the fruit mix for this (minus the flour and glaze) 24–48 hours in advance and let sit, covered in a cool place, for the flavours to infuse.

Serves 8

Prep Time: 30 minutes
Cooking Time: 5 minutes

800 g mixed dried fruit
100 g muntries
100 g riberries
100 g macadamias, chopped
1 teaspoon ground lemon myrtle
¼ cup Applewood Red Okar (native liqueur) or Campari or sherry
1½ cups Warndu herbal tea (your choice), coffee or fruit juice
2 cups self-raising flour
2 tablespoons bush jam, for glazing

Notes: Bush jam is really just any jam made with Australian ingredients.

The longer you leave the fruit to marinate, the better.

Riberries and muntries can be replaced with 2 cored and chopped apples.

In a large bowl, mix all the ingredients except the flour and jam and let sit for at least a few hours covered with a tea towel.

Preheat the oven to 130°C. Line a loaf tin or 20 cm square cake tin with baking paper.

Stir the flour into the fruit mix and pour into the lined tin. Tap the tin on the bench a few times to even out the batter. Bake on the bottom shelf of the oven for 2 hours.

Remove from the oven and use a pastry brush to glaze the cake with jam while still warm. Remove the cake from the tin after 10 minutes and allow to cool. Store in an airtight container once fully cooled.

Mince Pies

You will never buy a pack from the supermarket again once you try these. I would absolutely recommend making the mincemeat a few months before you make the pies for Christmas, so those amazing spices can infuse.

Makes 18

Prep Time: 20 minutes
Cooking Time: 20 minutes

For the filling:
400 g raisins
400 g dried muscatels
200 g dried apricots
100 g candied orange rind
100 g candied ginger
3 cups muntries
2 oranges, peel only and chopped finely
4 finger limes, caviar pearls and half
  the skin sliced finely
1 teaspoon ground cloves
200 g dried or fresh riberries
500 g firmly packed soft brown sugar
150 g chopped almonds or macadamias
2 teaspoons ground cinnamon myrtle
1 teaspoon ground anise myrtle
2 teaspoons ground lemon myrtle
1 tablespoon roasted ground wattleseed
1 teaspoon ground nutmeg
100 ml Applewood Red Okar (native
  liqueur) or orange liqueur such as
  Cointreau
125 ml brandy

To make the filling: Finely chop the raisins, muscatels, apricots, orange rind, ginger and muntries. In a large bowl, combine all the ingredients except the alcohol. Transfer to a greased large baking dish, cover and set aside for a few hours.

Preheat the oven to 100°C. Cover the mincemeat with baking paper and bake for 3–4 hours. Remove from the oven and cool, stirring regularly.

Once cool, stir in the alcohol and spoon the mixture into sterilised jars. Seal, label and store in a cool, dark place. Ideally, allow to mature for 3–12 months before using. You will need about 280 g of mincemeat for this recipe.

To make the pastry: In a large bowl, rub the grated butter into the flour. Mix in the sugar and a pinch of salt, and wattleseed. Combine the pastry into a large ball and knead it briefly; don't overknead. The dough will be fairly firm, like shortbread dough. You can use the dough immediately, or chill for later.

Preheat the oven to 180°C.

For the pastry:
225 g cold butter, grated
350 g plain flour
100 g raw caster sugar
pinch of salt
butter, for greasing
1 tablespoon roasted ground
   wattleseed
1 small free-range egg
raw caster sugar, for sprinkling
icing sugar, for dusting

Note: If you can't get muntries (native apples), use a Granny Smith apple.

Grease 18 holes of 2 x 12-hole small shallow pie tins with a little butter. Roll out the pastry and use a glass to cut out rounds just big enough to fit in the tins. Push the pastry rounds in gently. Spoon a heaped tablespoon of mincemeat into each pie.

To make lids for the pies, cut out rounds of pastry slightly smaller than before. If you like, you can cut out shapes such as stars instead or use thin slices of pastry to make lattice. Top the pies with their lids, pressing the edges gently together to seal; you don't need to seal them with milk or egg, as they will stick on their own.

Beat the egg and brush onto the tops of the pies to make them shiny. Sprinkle with a little sugar. Bake for 20 minutes, or until golden. Leave to cool in the tins for 5 minutes, then remove to a wire rack.

Once the pies are completely cool, lightly dust with icing sugar. They will keep for 3 or 4 days in an airtight container. Serve warm with cream, ice cream or brandy custard.

Love Cake

This is our version of a Persian love cake. It is chewy,
sweet and spicy. Best served warm with cream or ice cream, it will
keep in an airtight container for up to a week.

Serves 10

Prep Time: 15 minutes
Cooking Time: 1 hour

250 ml full-cream milk
1 teaspoon bicarbonate of soda
2 cups plain flour
2 teaspoons baking powder
1½ cups brown sugar
170 g butter, chilled and grated
1 large free-range egg
1½ teaspoons ground lemon myrtle
1 teaspoon ground anise myrtle
1 teaspoon ground cinnamon myrtle
1 teaspoon ground strawberry gum
1 teaspoon wattleseed extract
½ cup macadamia nuts, chopped
¼ cup marmalade or honey, warmed
dried edible flowers, for garnish

Preheat the oven to 170°C. Grease and line a 21 cm springform tin with baking paper.

In a small bowl, combine the milk and bicarbonate of soda and set aside.

Put the flour, baking powder, sugar and butter into a food processor and blitz until it looks like breadcrumbs. Transfer the mixture to the base of the tin, pushing down with your fingertips (like a cheesecake base). Set aside.

In another bowl, beat the egg with all the dried spices using an electric or stand mixer until light. Mix in the wattleseed extract and milk mixture. Pour over the base and sprinkle with the macadamias. Bake for 1 hour, or until a skewer comes out clean.

While still warm, brush with the marmalade or honey and sprinkle with dried flowers to garnish.

Bundy Bundt Cake

Don't eat this before picking up the kids from school.
I say that because 1. You won't stop at one piece and 2. It has a
considerable 'after breath' of Bundy. I think this cake is as good as
a cake can get, and is even better with a lot of cream.

Serves 8

Prep Time: 20 minutes
Cooking Time: 1 hour

2 cups plain flour
1 teaspoon bicarbonate of soda
pinch of salt
1 teaspoon ground anise myrtle
1 teaspoon ground cinnamon myrtle
1 teaspoon ground nutmeg
1½ cups brown sugar
½ cup macadamia oil
3 free-range eggs
½ cup full-cream milk
¼ cup Bundaberg rum
¾ cup chopped macadamias

For the rum glaze:
250 g butter
¼ cup filtered water
1 cup white sugar
1 cup Bundaberg rum

Preheat the oven to 180°C. Grease and flour a 25 cm ring (bundt) tin.

In a large bowl, mix together the flour, bicarbonate of soda, salt and spices. Set aside.

In a medium bowl, whisk together the brown sugar, oil, eggs, milk and ¼ cup rum until blended.

Make a well in the centre of the dry ingredients. Pour in the rum mixture and stir until combined. Add the macadamias and mix through.

Pour the mixture into the cake tin. Bake for 1 hour, or until a skewer inserted into the centre of the cake comes out clean. Allow to cool in the pan. Pierce the cake 15–20 times with a wooden skewer to prepare the cake for the rum glaze.

To make the rum glaze: In a saucepan, melt the butter in the water then bring to a slow boil. Stir in the sugar and continue to boil for 5 minutes, stirring constantly.

(continued over page)

Bundy Bundt Cake *(continued)*

Remove from heat and let cool for 5 minutes.

Stir in the rum. Let cool for 15 minutes.

Drizzle a small amount of the rum glaze over the top of the cake while it is still in the pan. Continue to drizzle glaze over until the top of the cake can't absorb any more glaze inside the holes. Turn the cake out of the pan and onto a plate, pierce the cake about 20 times across the base, then drizzle the glaze over the bottom of the cake until it can't absorb any more glaze.

Let the cake sit until the glaze has soaked in.

Put the cake back into the pan and reglaze the top. It may take 24 hours for the cake to completely absorb all of the rum glaze.

Aussie Bitters

Medicinal bitters are amazing for cold and flu season. They are best used as a preventative at the start of the season, taken for a week or so as a morning shot (approximately 30 ml). Bitters are also a great way to give yourself a big medicinal boost when energy is low, and are a wonderful digestif if you've had a big meal.

Makes 300 ml

Prep Time: 5 minutes
Wait Time: 6 weeks

2 finger limes
10 desert limes, halved
15 g rosella flowers
1 teaspoon whole pepperberry, crushed
1 tablespoon raw honey
2 sprigs sea rosemary, chopped
2 teaspoons ground anise myrtle,
   or 5 whole dried leaves
1 teaspoon ground native thyme,
   or 2 dried sprigs
250 ml brandy

Cut the limes in half. Put all the ingredients in a sterilised jar and seal. Shake until the honey is dissolved.

Store in a cool, dark place and shake every couple of days or so, for 6 weeks. Strain and store in a sterilised bottle. Use in drinks and cocktails or as a health shot when needed.

Wattleseed Honey Brew

We developed this recipe with our mate Scotty from Mischief Brew for our product range because it's delightful. But then it fermented (which made it even more delightful) and we couldn't be arsed with equipment to control it for sale, so we're just making it for ourselves. For now, anyway.

Makes 1 litre

Prep Time: 5 minutes
Wait Time: overnight

1 litre filtered water
15 g roasted ground wattleseed
25 g raw honey

Bring the water and wattleseed to the boil in a saucepan then reduce the heat to 80°C. Continue to boil at 80°C for a minimum of 1 hour. Reduce the temperature to 50°C and stir in the honey until dissolved.

Place into a sterilised bottle or jar and cool as quickly as possible in the fridge. Leave for 24 hours and then strain through a very fine sieve into another sterilised bottle. Leave in the fridge until ready to serve.

If you would like a fermented brew, leave out of the fridge in a food-grade plastic container (leaving room for expansion) for a few days until fermented to your liking.

Sandalwood, Rose, Boab & Coconut Granola

Granola is so much better when you make it yourself. I love the idea of cereal but totally freak out when I read the ingredients label – eek, the bad stuff! Do yourself a favour and make it yourself. Fifteen minutes on a Sunday and enjoy it every morning. Fresh, crunchy and no nasties.

Serves 10

Prep Time: 5 minutes
Cooking Time: 15 minutes

1½ cups shredded coconut
½ cup toasted macadamia nuts,
   roughly chopped
½ cup toasted sandalwood nuts,
   roughly chopped
⅛ cup chopped boab or 2 tablespoon
   ground
⅛ cup pepitas
⅛ cup sunflower seeds
¼ cup cacao nibs
3 tablespoons chia seeds
1 tablespoon ground raw cacao
1 tablespoon roasted ground
   wattleseed
1 teaspoon ground cinnamon myrtle
¼ cup coconut oil, melted
3 tablespoons maple syrup
1 tablespoon dried rose petals

Note: *You can use some bunya nuts in your mixed nuts!*

Preheat the oven to 150°C. Line 2 baking trays with baking paper and set aside.

In a large bowl, thoroughly mix together all the dry ingredients except the rose petals and ground boab, if using. Then stir in the oil and maple syrup.

Place the granola on the 2 baking trays, spacing the ingredients evenly and not on top of each other. Bake for 10–15 minutes, or until golden brown.

Remove from the oven and let cool completely. Stir through the rose petals, and ground boab if using. Store in an airtight jar for up to 2 weeks. This contains oil which may settle at the bottom of the jar.

Emu Egg Sponge Cake with Lemon Myrtle Cream

This recipe was given to me by the absolute legend of a high-school teacher, Cat Clarke. Cat is a 'Home Ec Queen' and has always championed Australian native produce with her hordes of teenagers, getting them educated young. Plus, she makes an epic cake!

Serves 8

Prep Time: 10 minutes
Cooking Time: 20 minutes

1 emu egg, or 6 hen eggs
⅔ cup caster sugar
1 teaspoon vanilla bean paste
1 cup self-raising flour
1 tablespoon ground wattleseed
finger lime or quandong jam (optional)
icing sugar, for dusting
yellow rose petals, to serve

For the lemon myrtle cream:
150 ml cream
1 teaspoon ground lemon myrtle
½ teaspoon vanilla bean paste or extract
2 tablespoons icing sugar

Preheat the oven to 170°C. Lightly grease 2 x 20 cm round cake tins.

Using a stand mixer with the whisk attachment, beat the eggs until pale and thick, about 5 minutes. Gradually mix in the sugar and vanilla. Remove the bowl from the stand mixer and sift in the flour and then add the wattleseed. Gently fold until combined. Pour into cake tins and bake for 16–18 minutes. Allow to cool in tins.

To make the lemon myrtle cream: In a bowl, whip the cream until medium peaks form. Stir through the lemon myrtle, vanilla and sugar.

Place 1 cake on a serving plate and dollop with jam and then lemon myrtle cream. Spread this on the bottom of the second cake. Place the second cake on top of the cream. Dust with icing sugar, top with extra jam and rose petals, and serve.

Orange, Sea Rosemary & Macadamia Self-saucing Pudding

Orange and rosemary are an absolute match made in heaven. Sea rosemary is stronger than European rosemary but, if you like a sweet/savoury taste, add an extra tablespoon.

Serves 6

Prep Time: 10 minutes
Cooking Time: 50 minutes

butter, for greasing
1 cup self-raising flour
1½ cups caster sugar
½ cup macadamia or almond meal
2 tablespoons finely chopped sea
  rosemary
1½ tablespoons finely grated orange
  zest, plus extra for the top (optional)
½ cup full-cream milk
1 large free-range egg
50 g butter, melted and cooled
1 tablespoon cornflour
2 cups freshly squeezed orange juice
flowers, for garnish
cream or ice cream, to serve

Preheat the oven to 180°C. Grease a medium-sized ovenproof dish with butter. Sift the flour into a large bowl. Stir in ½ cup of the sugar, the macadamia or almond meal, sea rosemary and orange zest. (I use a microplane to zest my oranges.)

In a jug, whisk the milk, egg and butter until combined. Add to the flour mixture and use a wooden spoon to stir until smooth and combined. Pour into the ovenproof dish and smooth the top. Zest a little more orange on the top of the pudding if you like to give more punch to your pud.

Combine the cornflour and remaining sugar for topping in a small bowl, then sprinkle over the pudding.

Place the orange juice in a small saucepan over medium heat. Bring just to the boil. Slowly pour the juice over the back of a spoon onto the pudding. Using the spoon stops the juice sinking into the mix.

Bake for 45–50 minutes, or until a cake-like top forms and a skewer inserted halfway into the centre of the pudding comes out clean. If you want it extra gooey in the centre, bake the pudding for 5 minutes less. Serve with lashings of cream or ice cream.

Citrus

Lemons and limes are a staple in cuisines the world over. While there is no native equivalent to the lemon or lime by way of large juice content, we certainly have a fabulous array of citrus that packs a tart and sour punch, including the finger lime, blood lime, desert lime and sunrise lime, as well as one of my favourites, lemon aspen (not technically citrus, it has a core like an apple). And they come in an array of stunning colours, shapes and sizes. Lemon aspen has a zingy lemony punch with a touch of pine and is a rich source of folate, iron and zinc.

Native limes occur in the warm regions of Queensland, New South Wales and South Australia. The most recognised and used would be the finger lime (Citrus australasica). Believed to be up to 18 million years old, this stunning evergreen species is endemic to the Queensland and New South Wales border area. Finger limes can be found on menus in some of the best restaurants all over the world. The fruit comes in a vast range of colours from reds to green, and has what has been dubbed 'finger lime caviar' in the centre – little tiny pops of pearly lime goodness. Plus, they are high in vitamin C, E, folate and potassium.

By far my favourite of them all is the Australian desert lime. Tiny with an intense flavour, it is like a sherbet bomb (a healthy one!). An extremely versatile fruit, it can be used in any product or process where standard limes or lemons are called for. Desert limes require no peeling or preparation and can be frozen without losing flavour or appeal when thawed.

If the native citruses in this chapter aren't available, substitute with standard limes and lemons; mix and match. Don't forget to use native limes in your drinks, too!

Desert Lime & Sea Rosemary Macadamia Cake

This, my friends, is bloody delicious, if I do say so myself. Easy to make, easier to eat in its entirety. Moist, buttery, sweet and sour all in one slice. Probably don't eat it all in one go!

Serves 8–10

Prep Time: 10 minutes
Cooking Time: 1 hour

4 free-range eggs
165 g caster sugar
180 ml macadamia oil
2 tablespoons finely chopped sea
  rosemary
100 g desert limes, finely chopped
225 g self-raising flour
½ teaspoon Murray River pink salt

For the icing:
120 g icing sugar, sifted
60 g butter, chilled and grated
60 ml lemon myrtle infused olive oil
  (or macadamia oil)
desert limes and sea rosemary,
  to garnish

Note: If you want a thicker layer of icing over the cake, double the icing recipe.

Preheat the oven to 160°C. Brush a 23 cm cake tin lightly with oil.

In a large bowl, beat the eggs for 30 seconds with an electric mixer. Add the sugar and beat until the mix is foamy, pale and increased in volume. While the mixer is still running, slowly drizzle in the macadamia oil until mixed in. Stir in the rosemary and lime.

In a separate bowl, sift the flour and stir in the salt. Using a low speed, mix the dry ingredients into the egg mix. Mix until combined.

Pour the batter into the tin and bake for 50 minutes, or until golden brown and a skewer inserted into the middle comes out clean. Allow to cool for 10 minutes in the tin, then turn out onto a wire rack to cool completely.

To make the icing: mix the icing sugar with the butter and oil to form a soft icing. Spread evenly over the cake. Decorate with sprigs of sea rosemary and limes.

Finger Lime Curd

If ever there was a curd that could make you pucker your lips in a good way, this one is it! This recipe is the most perfect combination of tang and tart. We love it on sourdough toast with lashings of butter. For a double tarty wham, top with sliced fresh desert limes.

Makes 500 ml

Prep Time: 5 minutes
Cooking Time: 50 minutes

125 g butter, cubed
1 cup raw sugar
2 finger lime skins, finely diced
½ cup finger lime caviar
   (you'll need about 10–15 finger limes)
4 free-range eggs, lightly beaten
2 teaspoons dried finger lime powder

Place the butter, sugar, finger lime skins and finger lime caviar in a heavy-based saucepan over low heat until the butter has melted and the sugar has dissolved. Remove from the heat and slowly beat in the eggs with a wooden spoon.

Return to low heat and stir until the mixture thickens, about 20 minutes. Do not boil or the eggs will curdle.

Remove from the heat and stir through the finger lime powder. Pour into sterilised jars, allow to cool to touch, seal and store in the fridge for up to 6 months.

Preserved Finger Limes

I always have leftover finger lime skins, as only a very small amount of zest is needed given their bitterness. So why not put them to good use and preserve them? The great thing about preserved finger lime skins is that when it comes time to use them in stews and tagines, you only need a small amount.

Makes 1 large jar

Prep Time: 5 minutes
Wait Time: 1 month

2–3 lemon myrtle leaves (optional)
20–30 finger limes, skins only
150 g Murray River pink salt
6 limes or lemons, juice and skins

Note: *You can also preserve any other native lemons and limes.*

Place the lemon myrtle leaves, if using, into a large sterilised jar. Stuff the finger lime skins with salt and pack into the jar tightly. Pour in the lime or lemon juice, then also pack the lime or lemon skins with salt and push them into the jar to use as a weight. Seal the jar and store in a cool, dark place for up to 2 years.

Dried Limes

These make wonderful additions to drinks, and are also good as decorations or even snacks. They are easier to slice when taken straight from the freezer.

Use any of the following:
finger limes
desert limes
blood limes
sunrise limes

Freeze the limes and then slice them super-thin when frozen.

Thaw the slices on paper towels until they're dry to touch. Then either put them into a dehydrator overnight or into an oven on the lowest temperature setting for 48 hours or until dried completely. If using a dehydrator, place them on 'Citrus' setting for 24 hours or until crispy dry. It's important to dry them out completely as any moisture will cause mould. Store in an airtight container for up to 1 year.

Boobialla Bitters

Boobialla is our very own native juniper berry. It has a distinct flavour and, mixed with a variety of other lovely herbs, has both medicinal benefits as well as a great digestif effect after a meal.

Makes 250 ml

Prep Time: 10 minutes
Wait Time: 6 weeks

6 finger limes
40 g boobialla berries
15 g dried whole rosella flowers
2 tablespoons coriander seeds
1 teaspoon ground native thyme
8 star anise
2 tablespoons ground anise myrtle
1 teaspoon ground lemon myrtle
1 teaspoon pepperberries
1–2 teaspoons honey
250 ml brandy

Place all the ingredients in a large sterilised jar, seal and shake well. Label and store in a cool, dark place for up to 6 weeks to infuse.

Strain into a sterilised jar. Use 1–2 tablespoons in your drink as a bitter flavouring. For a digestif, serve in a small glass or on ice.

Green Ant Citronello

I have loved limoncello for the longest time and this is my Aussie take on an Italian favourite. Best served ice-cold as a dessert wine, on crushed ice or in desserts.

Makes 2 litres

Prep Time: 15 minutes
Wait Time: 3 weeks

6 finger limes
5 blood limes
5 sunrise limes
20 desert limes
10 lemon aspen
1 litre vodka
1 g green ants
1 kg sugar
1 litre boiling water
strips of fresh citrus peel, to decorate

Note: For a citronello spritz, mix 1 part citronello with 4 parts soda or ginger beer, a handful of cocktail garden herbs, such as sea rosemary or river mint, perhaps some fresh finger lime and quandongs, or some citrus peels thinly sliced with the pith removed.

Slice all the citrus in half. Divide it between 4 x 500 ml sterilised jars. Cover evenly with vodka, add the ants and seal the jars, then shake to mix and leave for a week in a cool, dark place, shaking them a few times each day.

After a week, put the sugar into a heatproof bowl and pour over the boiling water, stirring until it is fully dissolved. Cool, then pour evenly into the citrus jars. Reseal the jars, shake and leave again for another week, shaking a few times a day.

After the second week, strain the liquid into decorative sterilised bottles. Citronello is best left to mature for a few months before drinking and will keep indefinitely. Decorate with strips of fresh citrus peel before serving.

Native Berry & Desert Lime Cordial

Fresh native berries come and go so quickly! It's not like they are all hanging out in the supermarket. These berries are rare and wild for the most part. Only a few suppliers grow them for sale. So when the season hits, get your hands on them and use them in every way you can.

Makes 1 litre

Prep Time: 5 minutes
Cooking Time: 10 minutes

750 g native berries
   (or a mixture of berry types)
750 g sugar
large handful of desert limes
4 tablespoons raw apple cider vinegar

Note: You can grow your own native raspberries at home. Get yourself some seedlings. We had them growing on our balcony in our apartment before we moved to the farm. Sure, we didn't get many berries but those we did get were pretty amazing!

For this recipe, you can use any of these: native raspberry, wild strawberry, riberry or lilly pilly. Riberry and lilly pilly are much easier to buy than the other berries. You may need to adjust the sugar according to your taste, as these fruits are very tart.

Place all the ingredients in a saucepan over a low heat. Mash the berries and cook for 10 minutes, until syrupy.

Push through a sieve into another clean saucepan. Put the fruit into a small bowl with about 600 ml water and mix. Strain that liquid into the pan with the syrup, trying to keep any seeds out of the syrup. Return the syrup to the heat and boil for 1–2 minutes.

Pour into a sterilised bottle and seal. Label and store for up to 3 months. Once open, keep refrigerated.

Lemon Myrtle & River Mint Gin Muddle

Here are a couple of gin cocktail recipes using the fine wares of two of our favourite gin makers: West Winds, and Applewood Distillery. Both of them use an array of amazingly blended Australian native herbs and spices to create unique gin that's as local as it gets.

Serves 1

Prep Time: 5 minutes

For the lemon myrtle sugar:
3 tablespoons raw sugar
6–8 lemon myrtle leaves
2 cm piece of lemon zest

For the gin cocktail:
3 tablespoons lemon myrtle sugar
1 lime wedge
60 ml Applewood gin
30 ml lime juice
2 sprigs of river mint
2 sprigs of lemon verbena

To make the lemon myrtle sugar: Grind the sugar, lemon myrtle and lemon zest in a spice grinder until fine.

To make the gin cocktail: Combine 3 tablespoons of the lemon myrtle sugar and 3 tablespoons of water in a small saucepan over medium heat and simmer until sugar dissolves. Refrigerate the syrup until ready to use.

Place the remaining lemon myrtle sugar on a small plate. Rub the lime wedge around the rim of a cocktail glass so that the sugar can stick to the glass, then dip the rim in the sugar; refrigerate the glass until ready to use.

Combine the gin, lime juice and 15 ml of the syrup in an ice-filled cocktail shaker. Shake well, then strain into the sugar-rimmed glass and garnish with sprigs of river mint and lemon verbena.

Wild Basil & Sea Rosemary Smash

So refreshing and packs a herby punch! You can make an alcohol-free version and it is just as delightful!

Serves 1

Prep Time: 5 minutes

2 sprigs of sea rosemary
1 bunch of wild basil leaves
25 ml lemon juice
15 ml sugar syrup
50 ml West Winds navy-strength gin
wild basil and sea rosemary leaves,
  for garnish
1 finger lime, sliced, for garnish

Place the sea rosemary, wild basil and lemon juice into a cocktail shaker. Gently smash the rosemary and basil. Add the sugar syrup and gin and top up with ice. Shake vigorously.

Double-strain into a glass filled with ice. Garnish with basil and sea rosemary leaves and finger lime slices.

Finger Lime & Lemon Myrtle Cheesecake

As the filling contains no gelatine, this cheesecake has a very soft set; if you prefer a firmer set, use 400 g of cream cheese and 150 ml of cream. The flavour combinations can very easily be played with. The base is crumbly so serve on the tin base or add more butter to the biscuit base.

Serves 8

Prep Time: 20 minutes
Fridge Time: 3 hours

For the base:
100 g ginger nut biscuits
150 g butternut snap cookies
50 g desert limes, finely diced, or the zest of 1 finger lime
1 teaspoon ground lemon myrtle
80 g butter, melted

For the topping:
340 g cream cheese, softened
200 ml cream (thickened or pure)
½ tablespoon roasted ground wattleseed
2 finger limes, caviar only, or 1 teaspoon dried
115 g raw caster sugar
juice and zest of ½ lemon

For decoration:
freeze-dried finger limes
crushed dried finger lime

Lightly grease a 23 cm springform tin.

To make the base: Crush the biscuits; either put them in a sealable bag and bash with a rolling pin, or use a mortar and pestle. I like chunky crumbs, but you can blitz them in a food processor if you prefer finer crumbs. Mix the finely diced lime or zest and lemon myrtle through the crumbs.

Melt the butter and mix it into the crumbs. Press the crumb mixture firmly into the base of the tin with your fingers. Put the tin in the fridge to set while you make the topping.

To make the topping: In a large mixing bowl, beat the cream cheese with an electric mixer just to loosen it, until it is the consistency of thickened cream. This should take no longer than 45–60 seconds. In a separate bowl, whip the cream. Fold the whipped cream into the cream cheese. Add the wattleseed, finger lime caviar, sugar, and lemon juice and zest, and mix until combined.

Spread the topping over the base using a spatula or knife. Put the cheesecake in the fridge to set for 3 hours. Decorate with freeze-dried finger lime and crushed dried finger lime.

Proteins

Meat. A highly contentious issue. One that can literally break a friendship, cause a fight, destroy our environment and, for some of us, make us drool – all at the same time!

Growing up, I was surrounded by sheep farms. I ate meat, I never asked where it came from. Not because I didn't care; I just didn't know to ask. I thought sheep, cows, chickens and pigs were it. That was our meat tray, so to speak – like the ones you win at the pub on a Friday night.

A few hundred years ago when Europeans rocked up on the shores of Australia, they brought a shipload of stuff with them. Noxious weeds, disease, racism, rules and, it turns out, a load of 'proteins' that have since ruined our ecosystem. Hoofed animals compacted the soils and ate the native plants. They did all this damage and yet there was already plenty of protein here, in kangaroo form.

I know, I know, kangaroos are super-sweet. Cute as a button. Our national emblem, on the fifty-cent coin and all that jazz. But the fact is, kangaroos have sustained our first peoples for thousands of years. Being light footed, kangaroos did no damage to the soils and didn't ruin our crops (before we made it impossible for them to find the food they used to eat). Kangaroo meat has virtually no saturated fat. Its levels of protein and zinc are similar to those of other meats, but it has more iron, twice as much vitamin B12 and higher levels of most other B vitamins. Kangaroo meat is 66 per cent of our daily protein needs per 150 gram serve and, when harvested correctly by reputable companies, the most ethical meat we can be eating.

Whatever protein you choose, make sure it's ethical, for the sake of our bodies and our planet. If you don't eat meat, no problem, just skip these recipes.

Kangaroo Leg with Dukkah

If you served this and didn't tell anyone what it was, they would swear it was beef! Tell them afterwards that it was Paroo Kangaroo. That's our trusted source for all our kangaroo meat!

Serves 12

Prep Time: 5 minutes
Fridge Time: 24 hours
Cooking Time: 1.5 hours

2 garlic cloves, crushed
2 cups Greek-style yoghurt
2 tablespoons ground lemon myrtle
salt and pepper, to taste
2.5 kg boneless kangaroo leg
200 g Warndu dukkah (see page 47)

Note: *This kangaroo leg can be barbecued instead of roasted. To do so, preheat barbecue to high. Reduce heat to medium and cook kangaroo, turning every 10 minutes for 40 minutes. Set aside to rest, loosely covered with foil, for 10 minutes before serving.*

Place garlic, yoghurt, lemon myrtle, salt and pepper in a large bowl and mix. Add the kangaroo leg and marinate in the fridge for 24 hours.

Remove the kangaroo leg from the marinade and set aside for 30 minutes at room temperature.

Preheat the oven to 180°C.

Place kangaroo leg on a large roasting tray. Roast for 1 hour. Reduce oven temperature to 160°C and roast for a further 30 minutes for medium meat. Cover and rest for 10 minutes.

Slice to serve and sprinkle with dukkah.

Kangaroo Tails Wrapped in Greens

This can be cooked on a fire or a barbecue – but where possible, we prefer fire. Wrap the tails in any of the hardier native greens and cook until the meat falls from the bone.

Serves 6

Prep Time: 5 minutes
Cooking Time: 3 hours

mixture of native greens
   (use any hardy greens – we used
   lemon myrtle, fish rushes and bush
   mint)
3 x 1 kg kangaroo tails
kitchen string, to tie

Lay the greens on a clean kitchen bench. Top with the kangaroo tails and tie the greens with kitchen string to secure them to the tails.

Heat a barbecue or fire until embers or coals are hot.

Add the kangaroo tails and cook, turning occasionally, for 2–3 hours, or until the meat is well charred and falling off the bone. Cover loosely with foil and rest for 10 minutes before serving.

Yabbies with Bush Tomato & Finger Lime Mayo

No need for prawns anymore – when in season, use yabbies
instead. They are fabulous and so easy to cook.

Serves 4

Prep Time: 10 minutes
Cooking Time: 10 minutes

1 tablespoon whole pepperberries
¼ cup Murray River pink salt
2–3 lemon myrtle leaves
1 kg yabbies

For the mayonnaise:
½ cup whole-egg mayonnaise
1 tablespoon dried ground bush tomato
2 finger limes, rind finely grated
salt and pepper, to taste

1 tablespoon dried ground bush
  tomato, extra
1 tablespoon Murray River pink salt,
  extra
samphire, to serve

Fill a large saucepan with water, add the pepperberries,
salt and lemon myrtle leaves. Bring to the boil. Add the
yabbies and cook for 6–8 minutes or until they change
colour. Drain and chill over ice.

To make the mayonnaise: mix whole-egg mayonnaise,
ground bush tomato and lime zest. Season with salt and
pepper and transfer to a serving bowl.

Mix the extra 1 tablespoon of ground bush tomato and 1
tablespoon of salt and transfer to a serving bowl.

Serve the yabbies with mayo, bush tomato infused salt
and samphire.

Kangaroo Carpaccio

Carpaccio is a really simple and super-impressive party pleaser.
All you need is a great piece of meat, acid, fat and a little sweetness to
make perfect mouthfuls of sweet, salty goodness. Traditionally done
with beef and lemon, I have mixed it up with a little Aussie native love.

Serves 4–6 as an entrée

Prep Time: 1 hour
Cooking Time: 10 minutes

1 kg kangaroo fillet or strip loin
drizzle of good-quality olive oil
salt and pepper, to taste
Warndu Native Thyme Oil, or any
    flavoured oil such as basil or lemon
Warndu Wattleseed Balsamic, or any
    balsamic glaze
juice of ½ lemon
4–6 finger limes, halved
100 g desert limes, halved or quartered
100 g muntries
native thyme leaves or micro herbs,
    for garnish

Note: *If you don't want to use kangaroo,
use venison or beef fillet.*

Take the meat out of your fridge an hour before cooking
to bring it to room temperature. Place on a plate and
drizzle both sides with olive oil, rubbing it evenly across
the meat.

Heat a large frypan until almost smoking. Place the fillet
into the pan and sear until golden brown on all sides.
You want to just sear it, not cook it. Remove the fillet
and leave it to rest until cool to touch.

Using a really sharp knife, slice the fillet as thinly as
possible. Arrange on a platter and season with salt and
pepper. Generously drizzle the thyme oil and balsamic
vinegar over the meat, followed by the lemon juice.
Squeeze out the finger lime caviar over the slices. The
caviar can be difficult to get out so if needed, squeeze
the limes.

Drizzle with more oil, sprinkle over the desert limes,
muntries and herbs to garnish.

Roo & Youlk San Choy Bau

This is one of those use-whatever-you-have-in-your-fridge recipes. Here is the base – feel free to swap things you don't have with what you do, or add various seasonal vegetables. It's a perfect mid-week feast.

Serves 4–6

Prep Time: 5 minutes
Cooking Time: 20 minutes

1 tablespoon macadamia oil
2 garlic cloves, crushed
3 cm piece of ginger, finely grated
500 g kangaroo mince
1 tablespoon soy sauce
2 tablespoons oyster sauce
2 shallots, thinly sliced
3 finger limes, caviar only
1 teaspoon sesame oil
2 spring onions, sliced thinly
200 g youlk, diced, or 1 carrot
1 corn cob, kernels only
200 g snow peas, sliced
100 g samphire
small handful of sea parsley, chopped
small handful of macadamias, chopped
8 large lettuce cups or leaves

Note: *This also works with pork, chicken, lamb or beef mince. For a twist, you can use cabbage leaves instead of lettuce. Just blanch them for 1 minute in boiling water then refresh in cold water.*

Heat the macadamia oil in a large frypan or wok over high heat. Add the garlic, ginger and mince and cook until browned. Add the sauces, shallots, finger lime, sesame oil, spring onions, youlk (or carrot) and corn kernels, and cook for another few minutes, or until the mince is cooked through.

Add the snow peas and samphire, and stir through. Garnish with sea parsley and macadamias.

To serve, put a few spoonfuls of filling into the lettuce cups or leaves and wrap.

Green Ant Butter

Anyone who knows us will know we love butter. The addition of the green ants gives a flavour bomb to the butter (they taste a little like coriander seed and citrus). It is so much fun to make your own butter, but if you don't have time, just buy some really good stuff and garnish generously with ants.

Makes 250 g

Prep Time: 10 minutes

250 ml pouring or double cream, at
  room temperature
10 g green ants
pinch of Murray River pink salt
1 litre jar and 1 large glass marble
bowl of ice and water

Note: *Make sure you get your ants*
from an ethical supplier that sources
them from the Larrakia people.

Put the cream, half the ants and salt into the jar and add the marble. Shake with the marble for about 3 minutes or until the cream looks softly whipped, then it will go stiff. Keep shaking until the buttermilk separates. Once it does, strain off the buttermilk (use it for something else).

Put the butter into the bowl of ice-cold water and use your hands to massage the remaining buttermilk out – you need to remove it all or it will sour the butter. Wash the butter a couple of times (by dipping in and out of the water) and mould into whatever shape you like. Roll in the remaining ants.

Place the butter in an airtight container or wrap in plastic wrap, and keep it in the fridge for up to a week.

Magpie Goose à l'Orange

This recipe takes duck à l'orange to the next level. Magpie goose is in every way one of the tastiest meats I have ever tried, like a cross between duck and wagyu beef. It has much smaller breasts than ducks, so sadly does not go as far, but this is quality over quantity.

Serves 2

Prep Time: 5 minutes
Cooking Time: 15 minutes

4 oranges
½ cup brown sugar
2 tablespoons water
4 tablespoons Maidenii vermouth or
   sherry
375 ml orange juice
2 shallots, minced
375 ml kangaroo or chicken stock
60 g butter
4 magpie goose breasts (skin on if
   possible)
salt and ground pepperberry, to season
mashed potato, blanched samphire and
   seablite, to serve

Zest the oranges and slice the flesh into segments, discarding any pith. Set aside.

Bring the sugar and water to the boil in a saucepan and cook for a few minutes until the syrup caramelises and begins to turn golden brown. Add the vermouth or sherry, orange juice, shallots and stock and simmer until the sauce reduces to about 1 cup. Add the butter, orange zest and segments. Stir through. Set aside.

Season the breasts with salt and pepperberry and heat a non-stick frypan until it's super-hot and smoking. Cook on high heat on each side for about 3–4 minutes, or until cooked to your liking (best served medium-rare). Rest for a couple of minutes and reheat the sauce. Serve on a bed of mashed potato with blanched samphire and seablite on the side.

Slow-cooked Roo Tail

One of Damien's Nana Barb's special recipes and a favourite among both our families. Kangaroo is a very important part of Adnyamathanha culture. Please suck the bones when you're done, as the marrow is delicious too.

Serves 4

Prep Time: 10 minutes
Cooking Time: 2 hours

2 kangaroo tails, skin off, cut
    into portions
olive oil, for coating
2 teaspoons Vegemite
salt and pepper, to taste
2 onions, quartered
3 carrots, chopped
4 small potatoes, scrubbed and halved
2 handfuls of warrigal greens
rice or lentils, to serve

Note: *You can buy kangaroo tail from Paroo Kangaroo already portioned.*

In a large pot with a lid, sear the meat over high heat on all sides with a little olive oil until brown (colour equals flavour); you will need to do this in batches. Cover with water, add the Vegemite and season with salt and pepper. Put the lid on and reduce heat to low. Cook until the meat begins to get tender, about 1.5–2 hours.

Add the veggies, and top with more water if needed.

Cook for another 15 minutes. Sprinkle with fresh warrigal greens and serve over rice or lentils.

Roo Meatballs & Lemon Myrtle Pasta

If you're a first time 'rooer' (kangaroo eater), this is a good place to start. So easy to make, and perfect with the homemade lemon myrtle pasta on page 208.

Serves 4–6

Prep Time: 1 hour 40 minutes
Cooking Time: 40 minutes

1 kg kangaroo mince
1 cup breadcrumbs
½ cup sea parsley, chopped
2 teaspoons chopped sea rosemary
2 free-range eggs
3 garlic cloves, crushed
½ cup grated Parmesan cheese, plus
    extra to serve
salt and pepper, to taste
oil, for frying
1 onion, diced
2 x 400 g tins tomatoes
500 ml passata
drizzle of wattleseed balsamic vinegar
splash of Worcestershire sauce
1 tablespoon barbecue sauce
1 bunch of wild basil, leaves picked
lemon myrtle pasta (see recipe page
    208), to serve

Start by making the meatballs. In a large bowl, combine the mince, breadcrumbs, sea parsley, sea rosemary, eggs, 2 garlic cloves, Parmesan, and salt and pepper. Roll into balls using about a tablespoon of mix at a time. Place on a tray and chill in the fridge for at least 1 hour.

Remove from the fridge 30 minutes before cooking and roll in a little oil prior to cooking. Heat a large frypan to high heat. Fry the meatballs in small batches until golden brown on all sides. Set aside.

To make the sauce: In a large saucepan over medium heat, cook the onion with a pinch of salt until soft. Add the remaining garlic clove and cook for another minute. Add the tomatoes and passata along with the balsamic vinegar, Worcestershire and barbecue sauces, and cook over medium-high heat until it begins to reduce, around about 20 minutes.

Return the meatballs to the pan with half the basil and cook for another 10 minutes. Serve with the pasta and the remaining basil and sprinkle with Parmesan.

Wallaby Shanks

This recipe can be made using kangaroo or wallaby shanks; both are equally delicious. Wallaby has a stronger, gamey flavour than kangaroo and the best place to get it is from the amazing peeps at Flinders Island Meats, who are ethical harvesters.

Serves 4

Prep Time: 15 minutes
Cooking Time: 2 hours

4 wallaby shanks
1 tablespoon plain flour
drizzle of olive oil
½ onion or 2 shallots, finely diced
2 garlic cloves
1 celery stalk
1 carrot
1 x 400 g tin tomatoes
500 ml kangaroo or beef stock
¼ cup red wine
2 tablespoons ground bush tomato
1 teaspoon native thyme, fresh and picked, or half the amount dried and ground
2 sprigs of sea rosemary
1 teaspoon ground pepperberries
2 large sprigs of fresh saltbush, chopped
mashed potato, to serve
sea parsley, for garnish

Note: *If not using wallaby or roo, this recipe works for lamb too.*

Wash and pat dry the shanks then coat in flour. Heat a large, heavy-based pot with lid over high heat. Brown the shanks on all sides. Remove from the pot and set aside.

Add the oil, onion, garlic, celery and carrot to the pot. Cook until soft. Add the tomatoes, stock, wine and all the spices except the sea parsley.

Put the shanks and any meat juices back in the pot, bring to the boil over high heat then reduce to a simmer. Put the lid on and cook for 1½–2 hours, or until the shanks fall from the bone. Serve with mash and a sea parsley garnish.

Pipis in Vermouth

Pipis have always been prized by Indigenous peoples. Goolwa Pipi Co are doing amazing work with the Ngarrindjeri people to not just put these amazing pipis on our plates but also in conserving, protecting and preserving the pristine environment of Coorong National Park. High fives!

Serves 4

Prep Time: 10 minutes
Cooking Time: 5 minutes

extra-virgin olive oil, for frying
3 garlic cloves, minced
1 kg well-washed pipis
2 ripe tomatoes, chopped
½ cup chopped sea parsley
1 small red chilli, diced
1 sprig of Geraldton wax, finely chopped
2 lemon myrtle leaves
1 cup Maidenii vermouth, cider or dry
   white wine
salt and pepper, to taste
knob of butter
crusty bread and butter, to serve

Note: *Make sure you wash the pipis thoroughly as they can get quite dirty and gritty inside.*

Place a large pot with a lid over medium heat, add a glug of olive oil and lightly fry the garlic cloves for about 30 seconds. Don't let it brown.

Add the pipis, tomatoes, sea parsley and chilli. Increase the heat to medium-high and stir for 1 minute.

Stir in the Geraldton wax, lemon myrtle leaves and alcohol. Put the lid on the pot and cook until the pipis open, about 3–4 minutes. Shake the pot often while cooking.

Season with salt and pepper, add the knob of butter, stir and serve with good crusty bread and butter.

Stuffed Murray Cod

I have tried this recipe with both barramundi and Murray cod and they both work a treat. Whichever fish you choose, keep the bones and make a broth using Geraldton wax and lemon myrtle as your aromatics. In this recipe, the fish is baked in the oven but it can also be wrapped in foil and cooked on a fire.

Serves 4–6

Prep Time: 10 minutes
Cooking Time: 45 minutes

2 lemons
60 ml olive oil
1 red chilli, diced
small bunch of sea parsley, chopped
salt, to taste
1 whole Murray cod, approx. 1–2 kg
4 sprigs Geraldton wax
2 spring onions, cut into 10 cm lengths
10 lemon myrtle leaves
3 sprigs seablite

For the greens, per person:
olive oil, for frying
2 garlic cloves, finely diced
1 small chilli, finely diced
2.5 cm piece of ginger, finely diced
salt and pepper, to taste
small handful of karkalla
handful of samphire
1 finger lime, caviar only

Preheat the oven to 180°C. Slice 1 lemon into rounds. Squeeze the juice of the other lemon into a small bowl and add the olive oil, chilli, sea parsley and a pinch of salt. Drizzle half of the oil mixture into the fish's cavity and set aside the rest.

Stuff the fish with the Geraldton wax, spring onion, lemon myrtle leaves, seablite and the lemon slices. Place on a large baking tray covered in enough foil to wrap the fish. Drizzle the remaining oil mix over the fish. Season with a little more salt, wrap with foil or soak paper bark in water for 15 minutes and use it to wrap the fish (tie it to secure). Bake for 45 minutes, or until the fish begins to flake. Check at 30 minutes. Remove from the oven and let rest for a few minutes while you prepare the greens.

To make the greens: Heat a wok over medium-high heat. Pour a good drizzle of olive oil in the pan, add the garlic, chilli and ginger, plus some salt and pepper to taste, and fry for 1–2 minutes. Add the karkalla and samphire, and very quickly stir-fry. Garnish with finger lime and serve with the fish.

Barramundi Fillets with Muntrie Salsa

The first time I ever ate barramundi was in the Kimberley and it's still to this day the most magical place I have ever been. The salsa in this recipe goes with any fish, pork and chicken.

Serves 2

Prep Time: 30 minutes
Cooking Time: 5 minutes

2 x 200 g barramundi fillets, skin on
salt, to taste
1 tablespoon olive oil, for frying

For the salsa:
150 g muntries
1 small red capsicum, finely diced
2 spring onions, thinly sliced
2 sprigs of seablite
juice of 1 small lemon
dash of apple cider vinegar
1 teaspoon local honey
3 tablespoons olive oil
salt and pepper, to taste

Remove the fish from the fridge about 30 minutes before cooking to bring it to room temperature. Pat dry the fillets with a paper towel. Using a very sharp knife, score the skin but not the flesh, making shallow long cuts the length of the fillets. Season each side with salt.

Heat the olive oil in a non-stick frypan over medium heat. Place the fillets skin side down in the pan, increase the heat to medium-high and cook for 3–4 minutes, or until the skin is golden brown. Turn the fillets over and cook for another 2 minutes, until just cooked through or to your liking. Remove from the pan and let the fish rest while you make the salsa.

To make the salsa: Place all the ingredients in a small bowl and mix thoroughly. Season with salt and pepper. Serve the barramundi on top of the salsa.

Marron Cocktail

If you haven't had marron before, your life is about to change forever. OMG it's the tastiest lobster-like creature you have ever eaten. It melts in your mouth. Cook the marron and slice before making them all retro 70s in this recipe.

Serves 4

Prep Time: 15 minutes

1 baby cos lettuce, washed, dried and pulled apart into leaves
1 mini radicchio, washed, dried and pulled apart into leaves
500–600 g cooked marron, tail on but shell off
sprinkle of Davidson's plum or bush tomato powder, for garnish
small handful of chives, chopped, for garnish

For the sauce:
4 tablespoons aïoli
3 tablespoons quandong or tomato chutney
1 teaspoon ground bush tomato
3 teaspoons Worcestershire sauce
2 teaspoons creamy horseradish
Tabasco sauce, to taste
squeeze of lemon juice
3 finger limes, caviar only
salt and pepper, to taste

To make the sauce: In a medium bowl, combine the aïoli, chutney, bush tomato, Worcestershire, horseradish, Tabasco, lemon juice and finger lime. Taste and season with salt and pepper to your liking.

Layer a few leaves of the cos and radicchio in serving glasses.

Dip the marron into the sauce and heavily coat. Place on top of the leaves. Sprinkle with a pinch of Davidson's plum or bush tomato powder and some chives. Place in the fridge until ready to serve.

Salt & Pepper Crocodile

Salt from our amazing saltbush, ground up and mixed with our native pepperberry – the very best of friends – rolled over crocodile and fried into crispy morsels of goodness. If you haven't eaten croc before, you're in for a treat. It is a little chewy if overcooked, so keep it quick.

Serves 2

Prep Time: 10 minutes
Cooking Time: 5 minutes

For the spice mix:
1 tablespoon Murray River pink salt
1 tablespoon ground saltbush
½ teaspoon ground pepperberry
½ teaspoon ground lemon myrtle

500 g crocodile fillet
½ cup self-raising flour
2 tablespoons macadamia oil
½ cup lukewarm water
1 cup cornflour
vegetable oil, for deep-frying

Note: *This recipe also works well with barramundi instead of crocodile.*

To make the spice mix: Mix the spices together and set aside in a bowl. Reserve some for garnish.

Slice the crocodile into pieces about 10 cm long by 1 cm thick.

In a large bowl, mix together the flour and macadamia oil. Pour in the water and mix to a kind of pancake batter. Add more water if needed.

Place the cornflour in another large, shallow bowl.

Dip the crocodile slices into the batter, shake off excess batter, then dip in the cornflour and shake off excess cornflour. Place the slices on a plate until they are all coated. If you like, you can double coat the slices, too.

Heat the oil in a wok until it reaches 165–170°C. Test by adding a teaspoon of batter to the hot oil and if it solidifies and goes brown, perfect. Cook the crocodile slices in small batches for 2–3 minutes or until golden brown. Don't overcrowd the wok. Use a slotted spoon to remove and place straight into the spice mix. Gently coat and set aside on some paper towel. Serve hot with a dusting of extra spice.

Sunday Roast Magpie Goose with all the Trimmings

Sunday roast is the best. When I lived in London, there were ten of us expats who would have a Sunday roast together every week. You cannot have a roast without the sides so in the following pages we have included a bunch of side dishes that go perfectly with the goose. Wish we'd had magpie goose in London!

Serves 2–4

Prep Time: 5 minutes
Cooking Time: 35 minutes

1–2 whole magpie geese
olive oil
salt and ground pepperberry, to taste
pepperberry leaves, for garnish

Preheat the oven to 220°C. Place the goose on a baking tray lined with baking paper, and drizzle olive oil over the skin. Sprinkle generously with salt and pepperberry. Rub it in so you reach all the corners and crevices. Place in the oven and bake until the skin is beautifully browned and crisp. This should take about 10 minutes.

By this time some of the fats should have begun to fall onto the tray. Use a spoon to scoop some of the liquid from the tray and baste the goose with it.

Reduce the heat to 160°C and continue to cook for another 25 minutes. Serve goose with pepperberry leaves as a garnish.

Herby Lemon Quinoa Side Stuffing

The goose is too small to stuff, but you can't have a roast bird without stuffing, so make it as a side dish.

Serves 2–4

Prep Time: 5 minutes
Cooking Time: 20 minutes

1 cup uncooked quinoa
drizzle of olive oil
2 sprigs of sage, finely chopped
1 sprig of sea rosemary, finely chopped
½ cup chopped macadamias
3 tablespoons raw apple cider vinegar
juice and zest of 1 lemon
½ bunch of sea parsley, chopped
¼ cup rehydrated riberry or quandong, finely chopped
salt and pepper, to taste

Cook the quinoa by covering with about 2.5 cm water in a saucepan and simmer until the water is absorbed, about 15–20 minutes. You may need to top up with a little more water during cooking. The quinoa will be translucent around the edges when cooked.

Place frypan over high heat and drizzle in a little oil. Add the sage, sea rosemary and macadamias. Cook for 1 minute, or until the sage goes a little crispy. Add the vinegar, let it sizzle, then quickly add the quinoa, lemon juice and a little more oil, and cook until the quinoa begins to get a little colour; a few minutes should suffice. Stir in the parsley, add fruit, season with salt and pepper, then add the lemon zest and mix through.

Ooray Plum Sauce

The only accompaniment for a goose, in our opinion, is plum. And the best plum of all is this one.

Serves 2–4

Prep Time: 5 minutes
Cooking Time: 1 hour

500 g ooray plums, washed and quartered, seeds removed
250 g caster sugar
1 star anise
3 cloves
1 teaspoon ground cinnamon myrtle
100 ml red wine
100 ml water
salt, to taste
knob of butter

Note: If you like a chunkier sauce, leave out the sieving step.

Place the plums in a saucepan with the sugar, star anise, cloves, cinnamon myrtle, wine and water. Simmer over the lowest heat for about 1 hour, or until the plums have completely disintegrated.

Push through a sieve, and discard the spices and the plum skins, seeds and any pulp.

Put the liquid back into the saucepan, bring to a simmer and reduce by half until thickened. Stir in salt to taste, and the butter, then pour into a jug for serving.

Anise Myrtle Roasted Beetroot

Beets and licorice are besties. Enough said.

Serves 4

Prep Time: 5 minutes
Cooking Time: 1 hour

4 large beetroots, whole
olive oil
¼ cup apple cider vinegar
salt and pepper, to taste
1 tablespoon ground anise myrtle
2 tablespoons wattleseed balsamic
   vinegar or balsamic glaze

Note: *Use ground lemon myrtle in the*
same quantities as the ground anise
myrtle if you don't like licorice.

Preheat the oven to 180°C.

Wash the beetroots, leave on the skin for added nutrients, and quarter them. Place in a shallow dish or baking tray lined with baking paper. Drizzle with a generous amount of olive oil, pour over the apple cider vinegar, and season with salt and pepper to taste. Mix with your hands so the beetroots are evenly covered. Sprinkle over half the anise myrtle, saving the other half for a garnish.

Bake for 45–55 minutes, depending on how you like the beetroots cooked. Beetroot can get quite dry so you may need to add a little more vinegar or oil halfway through cooking. This is also the time to drizzle the beetroots with wattleseed balsamic vinegar or balsamic glaze and sprinkle with the remaining anise myrtle.

Turmeric, Sea Rosemary & Garlic Carrots

Roasted carrots are such a great Sunday roast side. These make a fab leftovers snack, too.

Serves 4

Prep Time: 5 minutes
Cooking Time: 50 minutes

8–10 carrots
macadamia or lemon myrtle infused oil
2 cloves garlic
25 g fresh turmeric
25 g fresh ginger, peeled
salt and pepper, to taste
2 tablespoons raw honey
3 sprigs of sea rosemary
handful of macadamias, toasted and chopped

Preheat the oven to 180°C. Line a baking tray with baking paper.

Wash and chop the carrots lengthways, leaving on the skin for extra fibre and nutrients. Place them into a large bowl and drizzle with the oil.

Using a microplane, grate the garlic, turmeric and ginger over the carrots. If you don't love a ginger kick, use half the amount indicated. Add a little salt and pepper, the honey and sea rosemary. Mix with your hands so the carrots are evenly coated, and place on the tray.

Bake for 45–55 minutes, depending on how you like them cooked. Serve with chopped macadamias.

Chilli & Garlic Brussels Sprouts

The only way to get Damien to eat his Brussels sprouts!

Serves 4

Prep Time: 5 minutes
Cooking Time: 5 minutes

olive oil, for frying
1–2 cloves garlic, grated
20–30 Brussels sprouts,
   halved lengthways
1 small red chilli, finely diced
splash of raw apple cider vinegar
2 finger limes, caviar only
salt and pepper, to taste

Note: *Add some fried emu prosciutto
(page 139), chopped, instead of bacon.*

Place a large frypan over high heat, add a little olive oil and the garlic and mix through. When hot, add the Brussels sprouts, flat side down. Cook for 2 minutes, or until golden. Turn the sprouts over and cook for another 1–2 minutes, depending on how you like them cooked.

Add the chilli and a splash of vinegar. Mix through the finger lime caviar and season with salt and pepper.

Macadamia & Garlic Greens

Glorious greens. So much flavour and vitamins and minerals in this combination!

Serves 4

Prep Time: 2 minutes
Cooking Time: 5 minutes

macadamia oil, for frying
1–2 garlic cloves, grated
½ bunch of kale, roughly chopped
handful of warrigal greens
handful of karkalla
handful of samphire
splash of raw apple cider vinegar
salt and pepper, to taste
handful of macadamias, toasted
  and chopped

Place a large, shallow frypan over medium-high heat. Add a splash of oil and the garlic and kale. Mix through using tongs, making sure the garlic is not in one spot. Add the remaining greens. Continue to toss the greens for 1 minute. Add a splash of vinegar and a pinch of salt, then toss again. It is important to not overcook as wilted greens are not overly enjoyable and lose their vital nutrients. They only need 1–2 minutes in the pan.

Season with extra salt, to taste, and toss through the macadamias. Serve hot.

Minty Lemon Samphire

This recipe also works well with green beans and broad beans.

Serves 4

Prep Time: 5 minutes
Cooking Time: 5 minutes

salt and pepper, to taste
500 g samphire, green beans, or shelled
  broad beans
olive oil, for drizzling
juice and zest of 1 small lemon
½ bunch of river mint,
  leaves picked

Note: You can also use native thyme
(4 sprigs).

Fill a medium-sized saucepan with water, add a pinch of salt and bring to the boil. When the water is boiling, add the greens and boil for 3 minutes, or until they begin to float to the top and are a much brighter shade of green than they were before cooking. Strain the water through a colander and place the greens straight into a serving bowl.

Drizzle the greens with olive oil and the lemon juice. Season with salt and pepper to taste. Toss through the lemon zest and mint leaves and serve.

Emu Prosciutto

There is prosciutto, then there is emu prosciutto made by you! Impress your friends with this easy-to-make recipe. Mix and match your spices according to your favourite tastes – for example, sweet or spicy, or sweet *and* spicy. You can use the same method with kangaroo instead of emu.

Serves 2

Prep Time: 10 minutes
Wait Time: 9 days

250 g salt
1 tablespoon ground pepper leaf
1 teaspoon ground saltbush
400 g emu fillets
1 tablespoon ground pepperberries
3 teaspoons ground dried bush tomato
muslin, to wrap the fillets

Note: You can leave it in the fridge for 2 weeks and it will become jerky, which is also fabulous.

Combine the salt and pepper leaf. Mix in half of the saltbush and distribute half of the mixture between as many plastic wrap sheets as there are fillets. Lay the fillets on each pile of salt and pepper mix, and pour the remaining mix over each fillet. Carefully wrap each parcel tightly, making sure the salt and pepper and saltbush mix covers the fillet completely. Place the parcels onto a small plate and refrigerate for 24 hours. Turn the parcels over and refrigerate for another 24 hours.

Unwrap each fillet and wipe off the seasoning mixture.

Combine the pepperberries, remaining saltbush and bush tomato and roll the emu fillets in the mix. Wrap the fillets tightly in a sheet of muslin so there are 3 or 4 layers of muslin around them. Tightly wrap with kitchen string and place in the vegetable drawer of your fridge. Curing time will vary depending on the size of the fillets. After 2 days of salting, the size of the fillet reduces as it dries and cures, and after 1 week it should be firm to the touch yet still a little soft. You can always unwrap a fillet and slice it to check.

Kangaroo Pie with Bush Tomato Sauce

It couldn't get any more Australian if we tried. Pie, check.
Sauce, check. Kangaroo, check. We also make party-pie versions of
this. Aussie party, check.

Serves 6–8

Prep Time: 30 minutes
Cooking Time: 1 hour

500 g plain flour, plus extra for rolling
2 teaspoons roasted ground wattleseed
pinch of fine sea salt
280 g cold unsalted butter, cubed
2 large egg yolks
2 small eggs whisked with 2
    tablespoons milk, for egg wash

For the pie filling:
1 tablespoon olive oil
1 large brown onion, finely chopped
500 g kangaroo mince
1 tablespoon cornflour
¾ cup kangaroo or beef stock
½ cup Bush Tomato Sauce (see page 146)
3 tablespoons Worcestershire sauce
3 tablespoons barbecue sauce
1 bay leaf
1 lemon myrtle leaf
1 teaspoon Vegemite
2 x 400 g tins kidney beans, drained
salt and pepper, to taste
roasted wattleseed, for sprinkling

To make the pie pastry: In a food processor, blitz the flour, ground wattleseed and a pinch of salt together for a few seconds. Add the butter and blitz again until the mixture looks like coarse breadcrumbs. Whisk together the egg yolks and 3 tablespoons of water then mix in with the pastry until it forms a ball. Wrap the pastry in plastic wrap and leave it to rest in the fridge for at least 1 hour. Before using, remove the pastry from the fridge to bring it to room temperature.

To make the pie filling: Place a saucepan over medium heat, add the olive oil and onion and cook until soft. Increase the heat a little and add the mince, making sure to break it up into small bits. Cook until just browned, stirring with a wooden spoon often so it does not stick to the pan. Mix the cornflour and 1 tablespoon of stock to form a paste, add to mince, then slowly add the remaining stock. Add all the sauces, bay and lemon myrtle leaves, Vegemite and drained beans, and stir through. Bring to the boil. Reduce heat to medium-low and simmer for 5–10 minutes, or until thick. Remove the bay and lemon myrtle leaf, season with salt and pepper to taste, and set aside to cool while you prepare the pie dish.

Preheat the oven to 200°C or 180°C for fan-forced.
(continued over page)

Note: *You can make the pastry the day before, as long as you take it out of the fridge at least an hour before using to bring it to room temperature.*

Place a baking tray in the oven. Grease a 23 cm round by 5 cm deep pie dish with a little butter.

Once the pastry is at room temperature, roll it out thinly, to about 3–4 mm thickness, on a well-floured surface. Place into the pie dish. Always add an extra 1–2 cm overhang all round, as the pastry will shrink when baked. Then use the dish as a guide to cut out the pastry lid, again making sure you have an overhang on the lid too.

Place the pastry base in the dish, prick the base with a fork then spoon in the cooled filling so that it is level with the top of the dish. Don't overfill. Brush the pastry rim with a little egg wash, then drape the pastry lid over it, pinching the edges to seal. Make 4 tiny slashes in the centre of the lid, then brush with the egg wash.

Bake for 35–45 minutes, or until the pastry is golden brown. Reduce the heat by 10–20°C after about 20 minutes. Remove the pie from the oven and leave it to rest for about 10 minutes before cutting. Sprinkle with roasted wattleseed and serve with Bush Tomato Sauce.

Bush Tomato Sauce

This sauce has a wonderful savoury, caramelly flavour and also makes a wonderful pasta sauce.

Makes 500 ml

Prep Time: 5 minutes
Cooking Time: 15 minutes

4 tablespoons olive oil
4 garlic cloves, peeled and finely sliced
bunch of wild basil, leaves torn
3 x 400 g tins of good-quality,
  whole plum tomatoes
1 tablespoon brown sugar
3 sprigs of sea rosemary, chopped,
  leaves only, stems removed and
  discarded
4 tablespoons finely chopped bush
  tomato (about 20 dried bush tomatoes)
1 tablespoon apple cider vinegar
salt and freshly ground black pepper

Note: This is a quick sauce and is thin.
If you want a thicker sauce, simply keep
reducing it until you get the consistency
you are happy with.

Place a large non-stick frypan over medium heat and add the olive oil. Add the garlic, and once it begins to colour lightly, add the basil and tinned tomatoes. Using the back of a spoon, squash the tomatoes as much as you can. Stir in the sugar, rosemary, bush tomato and vinegar. Season with salt and pepper. Bring to the boil, then remove the pan from the heat.

Strain the sauce through a coarse sieve into a bowl, using a wooden spoon to push any larger bits of tomato through. Discard the basil and garlic that will be left in the sieve. Pour the sauce back into the pan, bring to the boil again, then reduce the heat and simmer for 5 minutes.

Allow to cool then store the sauce in a clean jar in the fridge – it'll keep for a week or so, and you can also freeze it in portions.

Aussie Bacon

Any pork eater needs to know how to make their own bacon. It is so gratifying to make it yourself and once you see how easy it is, you will be experimenting with your native herb and spice pantry.

Serves 6

Prep Time: 5 minutes
Wait Time: 2 days

1 tablespoon pepperberries, crushed
2 teaspoons dried boobialla berries (or juniper), crushed
1 teaspoon chilli flakes
2 teaspoons sea rosemary, finely chopped
1 teaspoon dried native thyme leaves
1 teaspoon roasted ground wattleseed
3 lemon myrtle leaves
2 bay leaves
3 tablespoons good-quality salt
60 ml raw honey
3 garlic cloves, crushed
2 tablespoons cold strong coffee or wattleseed brew (see page 69)
500 g pork belly

Use a mortar and pestle to crush all the spices (except the lemon myrtle and bay leaves) and tip into a bowl with the remaining ingredients except the pork. Mix together. Rub the mix over the pork belly, top and bottom. Place in a ziplock bag and squeeze out the air as you lock it.

Place in the fridge for 1 week and turn the bag over daily. Liquid will be drawn from the pork: this is good. After the seventh day, remove from the bag and wash the pork with cool water. Pat dry with paper towel and sit it on a wire rack over a tray in the fridge, uncovered, for a further 24 hours.

Preheat your oven to its lowest setting (70°C for most ovens), and cook the pork for 90 minutes straight on a rack with a tray underneath to catch any drips. Remove and allow to cool.

Keep the bacon in the fridge in an airtight container and slice as you need it. It will keep for 3 weeks in the fridge or in the freezer for up to 6 months.

Potted Murray Cod

We discovered some cool peeps called Red Earth Farms and love their work. Most people have been put off our native cod because of its muddiness, but these guys have figured out a way to ethically prepare them so they aren't so muddy, by growing them suspended from the bottom of the ponds.

Makes 4

Prep Time: 15 minutes
Cooking Time: 10 minutes
Fridge Time: 3 hours

butter, for greasing
400 g Murray cod fillets, skin on
splash of olive oil
salt and ground pepperberry, to taste
2 tablespoons finely chopped fennel
  fronds
1 heaped tablespoon salted capers
320 g unsalted butter, clarified
  and cooled
handful of samphire per person,
  washed and dried
splash of raw apple cider vinegar
crusty bread, to serve

Note: This also works with barramundi fillets or any flaking fish.

Butter 4 ramekins. Heat a frypan until smoking hot. Lightly coat the cod fillets with olive oil and season with salt. Cook the fillets, skin side down first, for 2 minutes. Flip and cook for another 2 minutes, or until the flesh begins to fall apart. Put into a bowl, remove the skin and discard it (or crisp up in the oven to use as a crisp bread) then flake the flesh into small pieces. Mix through the fennel, capers, and salt and pepperberry to taste.

Preheat the oven to 150°C. Divide the fish between the ramekins and press down to level the surface. Cover the fish with two-thirds of the clarified butter. Transfer the ramekins to a shallow ovenproof dish and add boiling water to come halfway up the sides of the ramekins. Bake for 10 minutes. Remove from oven and leave to cool.

Pour the remaining clarified butter over the fish until it is completely covered. Refrigerate the ramekins for at least 3 hours to set properly. Remove the potted cod from the fridge 20 minutes before serving to bring it back to room temperature. Serve straight from the pots or turn onto a plate so the butter layer is underneath.

Just before serving, slice the samphire, splash with apple cider vinegar and sprinkle with salt and pepper. Serve the potted cod with the samphire and crusty bread.

Barra Hash with Horseradish Dressing

When you have leftover fish, or any leftover anything, really,
this is a great weekend breakfast go-to. This recipe can be made
with sweet potatoes too.

Serves 2–4

Prep Time: 5 minutes
Cooking Time: 10 minutes

2 tablespoons olive oil
400 g potatoes, cubed, boiled and
  cooled
1 tablespoon butter
1 shallot, finely diced
100 g boneless barramundi, flaked
¼ cup cream
1 garlic clove, finely chopped
¼ teaspoon ground pepperberry
2 tablespoons dill, finely chopped
salt and pepper, to taste
2 tablespoons crème fraîche
2 teaspoons grated fresh horseradish
handful of garlic chives, finely chopped
1 lemon, sliced into wedges

Note: *Use any leftover Murray Cod from*
page 122.

Place a frypan over medium heat, add the olive oil
and cook the potatoes for about 6–8 minutes, or until
starting to brown. Add the butter, shallot, fish, cream,
garlic, pepperberry, half the dill, and salt and pepper
to taste. Cook for about 10 minutes, mixing and turning
every couple of minutes so it does not stick.

Make the dressing by mixing the crème fraîche with
the horseradish, chives and remaining dill. Serve with
lemon wedges.

Bush Tomato Chicken Wings with Native Thyme Chips

This is Saturday night dinner in front of Netflix (or the footy).
Chicken and chips are a favourite in our house and these wings
are just as good cold the next day, if there are ever any left. Also
perfect for a picnic.

Serves 4

Prep Time: 10 minutes
Fridge Time: 2 hours
Cooking Time: 1 hour

1 kg free-range chicken wings
3 tablespoons olive oil
2 tablespoons ground bush tomato
2–3 garlic cloves, crushed
1 teaspoon Murray River pink salt
1 teaspoon ground lemon myrtle
2 teaspoons ground native thyme
1 teaspoon ground pepperberries
1 tablespoon soy sauce
1 tablespoon maple syrup
2 finger limes, caviar only
juice of 1 lemon

For the native thyme chips:
4 potatoes, washed, with skin on
½ tablespoon olive or Warndu native
  thyme oil
½ tablespoon lemon myrtle oil or ½
  teaspoon ground lemon myrtle
2 sprigs of native thyme or 1 teaspoon
  ground native thyme
salt and ground pepperberry, to taste

To make the wings: Wash and dry the chicken wings and place in a large bowl. Add all the remaining ingredients and mix thoroughly, making sure the marinade is all over the wings and in all of the crevices. Cover and leave in the fridge for at least 2 hours, or preferably overnight.

Remove the wings an hour before cooking to come to room temperature. Preheat the oven to 180°C.

Put the wings on 2 baking dishes or trays then, with your hands, coat the wings in the marinade again. Bake for 45 minutes to 1 hour, turning once or twice.

To make the native thyme chips: Slice the potatoes into chip lengths. Put into a large pot, cover with cold water and add a pinch of salt. Boil until just parboiled and soft to touch. Strain and shake in a colander until fluffy. Place the chips on a baking tray, add the oils, spices, salt and pepperberry, and mix so they are coated thoroughly. Bake in the oven with the wings for the final 30 minutes, or until golden brown.

Vegemite & Emu Egg Omelette

Emu egg shells are naturally green in colour; the shade varies depending on what the emu eats and the environment, ranging from a beautiful turquoise green to dark green (almost black). The eggs usually weigh about 600–700 grams, so make sure you are hungry.

Serves 2

Prep Time: 2 minutes
Cooking Time: 5 minutes

1 emu egg
½ teaspoon ground bush tomato
½ teaspoon Vegemite
½ knob of butter
1 spring onion, sliced
½ handful of sea parsley, chopped
1 tablespoon grated Parmesan cheese
1 tablespoon pouring cream
small handful of warrigal greens
½ chilli, finely sliced (optional)
salt and ground pepperberry, to taste

Note: This recipe works well with duck or hen eggs.

In a mixing bowl, crack the emu egg and whisk until frothy. Stir through the bush tomato and Vegemite.

Heat a medium frypan over medium heat and melt the butter. Once frothy, pour in the egg mixture. Quickly stir using an egg slice, then add the spring onion, sea parsley, Parmesan, cream, warrigal greens and chilli, if using.

Keep stirring until you get the consistency you like in an omelette. I prefer them just set, which takes about a minute and a half. Season with salt and pepperberry.

Native Oysters with Finger Lime & Seablite

Simple, fresh, zingy. Nothing more needed –
except perhaps a cold glass of bubbles.

Prep Time: 5 minutes

oysters
fresh finger limes
seablite
sea parsley

Use any native Australian oyster here. Shuck oysters
and garnish with half a finger lime and small sprigs of
seablite and sea parsley.

Quandong (Urti) Roast Pork

This recipe uses our hero, the quandong, which is our native peach.
Its tangy, sour flavour complements the fatty pork –
a match made in heaven.

Serves 6

Prep Time: 10 minutes
Cooking Time: 1 hour 40 minutes

500 g fresh or dried quandongs, halved
  and seeds removed
1.5 kg pork leg or shoulder with rind
  (free-range or ethically sourced)
4 tablespoons olive oil
salt, to taste
1 teaspoon ground anise myrtle
1 onion, peeled and halved
2 large fennel bulbs, halved
2 teaspoons plain flour
1 cup dry cider, Maidenii vermouth or
  Applewood Red Okar (native liqueur)
500 ml chicken or kangaroo stock

Preheat the oven to 220°C. If using dried quandongs, rehydrate them by covering with cold water in a bowl and setting aside to soak.

Take the pork out of the fridge an hour before cooking to bring it to room temperature. Pat dry with paper towel and score the rind of the pork with a sharp knife. Score across the rind, a finger-width apart, then back the other way. Cut only halfway down into the fat. Rub the rind with olive oil and sprinkle with a generous amount of salt. Push the anise myrtle into the cuts evenly. Place the pork in a large roasting tin, tucking the onion and fennel under it.

Roast the pork for 1 hour and 40 minutes. Remove the pork from the roasting tin, place on a board and cover loosely with foil. Leave to rest for 20 minutes.

To make the sauce: Put the roasting tin over high heat on the stovetop, removing the onion and fennel. Bring the juices to a low boil, then mix in the flour. Pour in the alcohol and add the quandongs. Stir constantly, as the sauce begins to reduce quickly. Add the stock and simmer for about 10 minutes. Serve the sauce over the sliced pork.

Fruits & Flowers

Quandongs (native peaches) or 'urti' (pronounced *oo-ti* in Damien's language) are a very important part of Damien's culture. They are local to the Flinders Ranges, Damien's yarta (country). Some of his earliest memories are of gathering them as a kid with his pop. In fact, every year there's still great excitement among his family members when the fruits begin to turn their many shades of pink and red. Damien's mum and dad fill bags of the fruit for us from their own trees and trees in secret places, and stuff the freezer full to the brim for safekeeping when the urti season ends.

There are literally hundreds of Australian native fruits found on vines, shrubs, bushes and trees. During different times of the year, these fruits are part of the staple diet of different Aboriginal communities. Unlike our supermarket shelves these days, stocked with strawberries and pineapples in winter, native fruits have an extremely short season and their availability is intermittent.

To truly appreciate native fruits we need to adjust our expectations to accommodate bitterness, acidity and a high amount of sourness. These fruits aren't eaten as snacks every day; they are a treat and a seasonal break in the diet. Many of them are picked as medicine, like the mighty powerful Kakadu plum, which has one of the highest concentrations of vitamin C on the planet.

Like all Australian native foods, fruits have their own local Indigenous language name depending on what area they come from, but they have colloquial names, too, and many of them are simply referred to as 'wild' or 'native' apple, peach, etc. It can be confusing, so it's best to always try and get the botanical name of any native plant food.

The fruits and flowers of our backyard are pure beauty. While challenging on the palate at times, they truly blow your mind and open it to the possibility of a whole other flavour profile you didn't even know existed. When possible, get them fresh, and if not, frozen or dried.

Pickled Rainforest Cherries

It is well worth making pickled cherries when they are in season and stocking up your pantry with them for your cheeseboards and Christmas turkey as an alternative to cranberry sauce.

Serves 10

Prep Time: 30 minutes
Cooking Time: 5 minutes

1 kg rainforest cherries (thawed)
6 strips orange zest
350 g caster or brown sugar
500 ml white wine vinegar or apple
   cider vinegar
180 ml water
10 cloves
1 teaspoon ground lemon myrtle
1 teaspoon ground anise myrtle
1 teaspoon ground cinnamon myrtle
2 cm piece of ginger, smashed
6 cardamon pods, bruised

Note: Can be purchased frozen outside of their season. Any fresh cherry can be substituted in this recipe.

Wash the cherries. Keep the cherries as whole as possible.

Combine all the ingredients except the cherries in a saucepan, bring to the boil and then simmer for 20 minutes.

Pack the cherries into sterilised jars and pour over liquid. Place in a cool, dark place; can be stored for up to 1 year.

Pickled Rainforest Cherry Chocolate Pie

This is as decadent as it gets and ticks every pie box possible.
Rainforest cherries are amazing. They are perfect for this recipe
but if you can't get them you can use any other cherry.

Serves 8

Prep Time: 30 minutes
Cooking Time: 5 minutes

For the chocolate pie crust:
2½ cups plain flour
2 tablespoons raw cacao or cocoa
   powder
1 tablespoon roasted ground wattleseed
1 teaspoon icing sugar
pinch of salt
1 cup butter, chilled and grated, plus
   extra for greasing
100–125 ml cold water
small handful of almonds or other nuts
½ teaspoon ground mixed spice or
   cinnamon
1 tablespoon honey

For the blind baking:
small handful of almonds or other nuts
½ teaspoon ground mixed spice or
   cinnamon
1 tablespoon honey

(continued over page)

To make the pie crust: In a food processor, pulse the flour, cacao, wattleseed, sugar and salt. Add the butter and pulse until the mixture resembles breadcrumbs. Add a little water (1 tablespoon at a time) and pulse again. Continue adding the water and pulsing, until the dough holds together when you squeeze it. Do not overmix. Turn out the dough onto some plastic wrap and knead into a disc shape. Place in the fridge for an hour.

Preheat the oven to 180°C. Grease a 19 cm flan tin with butter.

Roll out the pastry so it fits into your flan tin with enough to hang over the sides, as pastry always shrinks. (Trick: wrap the pastry around your rolling pin and unroll over the dish, gently pushing the pastry into the sides of the dish.) Prick the pastry a few times around the base with a fork. Any leftover pastry can be frozen.

To blind bake your pie crust: Place a piece of baking paper over the pastry and fill it with some almonds, a sprinkle of spice and a drizzle of honey, which you can use for a snack later. Bake for 10–15 minutes, or until the crust begins to go golden brown. If any of the pastry puffs, prick with a fork a little more.
(continued over page)

For the cherry filling:
250 ml cream
1 tablespoon icing sugar
1 tablespoon roasted ground wattleseed
zest of 1 orange
750 g jar pickled cherries (see recipe
    page 161) or 900 g native cherries
2 tablespoons brown sugar
1 teaspoon mixed spice

Remove the paper and almonds, and place the crust back in the oven for a further 5–8 minutes, or until the base is cooked. Remove from the oven and let cool before filling.

To make the cherry filling: Pour the cream into a mixing bowl. Add the icing sugar and wattleseed and mix with an electric hand mixer until thick enough that it won't fall off a spoon. You can add more or less icing sugar to taste. Mix in the orange zest.

If using pickled cherries: Use a slotted spoon to remove cherries from the juice and fold into the cream ever so lightly.

If using frozen or tinned cherries: Thaw frozen cherries or drain half of the liquid from the tinned cherries. Place the cherries in a bowl, add the brown sugar and mixed spice, and stir until the sugar dissolves. Use a slotted spoon to fold the cherries through the cream. You can drizzle in a little juice, too.

Fill the pie crust with the cherry filling. If you like, drizzle a little cherry juice on top for garnish, but not too much or it will go soggy. If you would like a sweeter filling, sprinkle the cherries with some brown sugar.

Fig & Quandong Chutney

Figs and quandong go superbly together. You can, of course, use ripe figs but often they just don't all ripen on the tree so this is a great way to use them all up. The quandongs add a beautiful tartness to this chutney, wonderful matched with creamy cheeses.

Makes 4 jars

Prep Time: 20 minutes
Cooking Time: 2 hours

500 g unripe figs
500 g quandongs, fresh or dried
500 ml raw apple cider vinegar
500 ml malt vinegar
250 g soft brown sugar
500 g brown onions
125 g crystallised ginger (you can use fresh ginger, 3 cm length, peeled and diced finely)
175 g honey
2 tablespoons salt
1 tablespoon cardamom seeds, bruised
1 teaspoon freshly ground pepperberry
1 teaspoon ground anise myrtle

Wash the figs and pat dry. Cut off and discard their tops, and cut the fruit into quarters. Wash the quandongs, remove stones and cut the fruit into quarters. If using dried quandongs, rehydrate them in water for an hour first.

Combine the figs, quandongs, vinegars and sugar in a large, heavy-based saucepan. Place over low heat and stir until the sugar is dissolved. Add the remaining ingredients and bring to the boil, then simmer for 1–2 hours, or until the figs are tender and falling apart.

Pour into 4 x 500 ml sterilised jars, seal and allow to cool. Label and store in a cool, dark place for up to 3 years. For the best flavour, let the chutney mature for at least 3 months before eating it. Refrigerate after opening.

Quandong, Muntrie & Cinnamon Myrtle Fruit Leather

Kids' lunch box snack. Adults' lunch box snack. Anyone's snack.
Make, store and chew.

Makes 8–10

Prep Time: 5 minutes
Cooking Time: 1 hour

400 g muntries
4 tablespoons dried quandongs
3 bush apples, peeled, de-seeded and
    diced
50 g raw honey
splash of rosewater
pinch of ground cinnamon myrtle, or
    ground lemon myrtle

If muntries aren't available, peel and core cooking apples, then dice them. Cook by simmering in a small saucepan of water until they are just soft. At the same time, put the quandongs in a separate small saucepan, cover with a small amount of water and simmer until soft, about 10–15 minutes. Add the bush apples to the muntrie/apple pot and simmer for about 5 minutes.

Once cooked, squeeze the quandongs through a piece of muslin into a food processor. Add all the cooked muntries/apples, honey, rosewater and cinnamon myrtle and process until smooth.

Preheat the oven to 110°C and line a baking tray with baking paper. Spoon the mixture into small, paper-thin circles on the baking tray, then bake for 1 hour, or until they are bendy; if you prefer crisp, then bake a little longer.

Remove from the oven and leave to cool completely on the baking tray, then carefully peel each circle off the paper. Store in an airtight container, with baking paper between each layer, for up to 1 week.

Wild Raspberry Jam

Rubus probus is our beautiful native raspberry. It is pretty rare, unless you grow your own, which is very easy to do. We had one growing on the tiny balcony of an apartment! They are a stunning fruit, so get your hands on a seedling or two.

Makes 1 litre

Prep Time: 5 minutes
Cooking Time: 20 minutes

1.3 kg native raspberries
1 kg sugar
juice of ½ lemon

Note: *You can add 1 teaspoon lemon, anise, cinnamon myrtle or strawberry gum.*

Wash the raspberries gently.

Warm the sugar in a low oven for 10 minutes.

Place the berries in a heavy-based saucepan over a low-medium heat. No water is needed. Cook for a few minutes until very soft, stirring so they don't catch and burn. Mash the berries with a potato masher. Stir through the warmed sugar and lemon juice and cook for 20 minutes, or until the jam is glossy and has reached setting stage.

Test the mixture by putting a small saucer in the freezer for 1 minute. Remove from the freezer and put 1 teaspoon of jam onto the saucer. Leave for 1 minute, run your finger through the centre of the jam and if it wrinkles it's set.

Place in 4 x 250 ml sterilised jars and seal. Store in a cool, dark place for up to 1 year.

Davidson's Plum & Cinnamon Myrtle Jam

Another one of those combinations that just cannot be beaten is plum and cinnamon. These native plums are really tart, so if you prefer you could use half native and half common plums, such as Victoria, greengage or red, or whatever is available from your neighbourhood trees.

Makes 1.5 litres

Prep Time: 10 minutes
Cooking Time: 1 hour

1 kg Davidson's, ooray or Illawarra
   plums
1 kg white sugar
zest and juice of 1 lemon
2 teaspoons ground cinnamon myrtle or
   4 leaves whole and crushed slightly

Wash the plums, halve them and remove the seeds. Weigh the fruit and make sure you have exactly the same amount of sugar as fruit.

Place the plums and sugar in a large, heavy-based saucepan. Add the lemon zest, juice and cinnamon myrtle. Heat on low, stirring until the sugar dissolves. Bring to a light rolling boil and allow to simmer for 1 hour, or until the mixture has slightly thickened.

Test the mixture by putting a small saucer in the freezer for 1 minute. Remove from the freezer and put 1 teaspoon of jam onto the saucer. Leave for 1 minute, run your finger through the centre of the jam and if it wrinkles it's set.

Once set, pour the jam into 4 x 250 ml sterilised jars and seal. Store in a cool, dark place for up to 2 years.

Pear, Plum & Preserved Finger Lime Chutney

I would use a mixture of native plums here, like Illawarra, ooray and Davidson's. This is a great one for the cheese board, as well as heated up as a sauce for meat and vegetables.

Makes 1.5–2 litres

Prep Time: 10 minutes
Cooking Time: 1 hour

250 g red onions, diced
200 ml red wine vinegar
150 ml raw apple cider vinegar
350 g sugar
1 kg native plums, like Illawarra or ooray
500 g pears
40 g preserved finger limes (see page 83), finely sliced
1 teaspoon finely ground pepperberry
1 teaspoon ground cinnamon myrtle
1 teaspoon mixed spice
1 teaspoon salt

Put the onions in a large, heavy-based saucepan over high heat with the vinegars and sugar. Once boiling, reduce the heat and gently simmer, stirring occasionally, for about 10 minutes, or until the onions soften and become shiny.

Wash the plums, remove stones and dice the flesh. Wash the pears, core and chop into small pieces. Add the fruit to the pan with the preserved limes, spices and salt. Bring back to the boil, then reduce the heat to a simmer and stir occasionally so that it doesn't stick to the bottom and burn. Continue to cook over low heat for 1 hour, or until the mixture becomes thick and has reduced by one-third.

Pour into 4 x 500 ml sterilised jars, seal and allow to cool. Label and store in a cool, dark place for up to 1 year. Refrigerate after opening.

Muntrie, Boonjie Tamarind & Emu Prosciutto Salad

This is our take on the prosciutto and peach salad. You can of course add mozzarella or burratta if you like.

Serves 2

Prep Time: 5 minutes

150 g boonjie tamarind, chopped
2 tablespoons raw honey
¼ cup boiling water
450 g emu prosciutto, thinly sliced
(see page 139)
100 g quandongs, thinly sliced
200 g fresh or frozen muntries, thawed
200 g samphire
200 g warrigal greens
1 tablespoon Warndu Wattleseed
Balsamic, or candied balsamic
vinegar
olive oil, to taste
salt and pepper, to taste

Place tamarind, honey and water in a small heatproof bowl. Set aside for 10 minutes, then strain and reserve the liquid.

Toss all the remaining ingredients together. Drizzle with 1 tablespoon reserved tamarind liquid, balsamic vinegar and olive oil to taste. Season with salt and pepper and serve.

Tamarind & Thyme Crème Brûlée

Wowzers. Next Level. Epic. Our favourite. Yummo.
Our version of rhubarb and custard.

Serves 4

Prep Time: 10 minutes
Cooking Time: 30 minutes

250 g boonjie tamarind, chopped
1 cup caster sugar
¼ cup water
¼ cup orange juice
500 ml double cream
1 teaspoon vanilla essence
6 sprigs of native thyme
6 egg yolks
⅓ cup caster sugar, extra, for sprinkling
2 sprigs native thyme, for garnish
   (optional)

Note: If you don't have a kitchen blowtorch, preheat oven grill to high. Place ramekins under grill for 30 seconds to 1 minute, or until tops are golden and caramelised.

Preheat oven to 180°C. Place tamarind, ½ cup sugar, the water and orange juice in a small saucepan over high heat. Bring to the boil. Reduce heat to medium and cook for 18–20 minutes, stirring occasionally, until the consistency is thick and jammy.

Spoon into the base of 4 x ¾ cup heat-proof ramekins or dishes. Place cream, vanilla essence and thyme sprigs in a medium saucepan over high heat. Bring to the boil. Reduce heat and simmer for 5 minutes. Remove thyme.

Place egg yolks and the remaining sugar together in a bowl and whisk. Pour cream mixture into egg mixture and whisk. Pour back into the saucepan, heat over low heat and cook for 4 minutes or until thick.

Carefully pour into ramekins. Place in a baking dish and pour boiling water into the baking dish to about halfway up the ramekins. Bake for 15–20 minutes, or until just set. (The brûlée should have a slight wobble.)

Cool at room temperature. Refrigerate for 2 hours or until cold. Sprinkle with extra sugar and torch the tops with a kitchen blowtorch until golden and caramelised. Serve immediately.

Quandong Iced Tea

For our grannies and grandpas, who drank all of the tea all of the time.

Makes 1 litre

Prep Time: 5 minutes
Wait Time: overnight

1 litre strong black tea (use 4 teabags)
honey, to sweeten (about 2 tablespoons)
10 quandongs, halved, stones removed
3 lemon myrtle leaves
ice, to serve
fresh quandongs and lemon myrtle,
   for garnish

Make black tea in a jug, stir in honey and add the halved quandongs and lemon myrtle leaves.

Leave overnight, covered, to infuse.

When ready to serve, strain, pour over ice and garnish with fresh quandongs and lemon myrtle.

The tea will keep for a week, covered, in the refrigerator.

Urti Pie

This recipe is so special to us as it comes from Damien's Nana Barb, who has since passed away. Most of Damien's family members make this pie, which is renowned in the Flinders Ranges, home of the urti (quandong). So when we make this pie, it's in Nana Barb's honour. She had a real sweet tooth!

Serves 6–8

Prep Time: 15 minutes
Cooking Time: 40 minutes

For the pastry:
2 cups (300 g) self-raising flour
1 cup (150 g) plain flour
200 g butter, chilled and chopped
125 ml iced water
pinch of salt
sugar, for sprinkling on pastry top

For the filling:
500 g fresh (or frozen and thawed) quandong, for sprinkling
¾ cup caster sugar, plus extra
1 cup water (just enough to cover the quandong) or orange juice
1 egg, beaten
2 tablespoons cream

Combine the fruit with the sugar and orange juice, stir, cover and let stand for at least five minutes, or, if you have time, leave overnight. This will create a thicker filling.

Transfer the quandong mixture to a saucepan and cook on low for 10–15 minutes, stirring frequently.

Preheat oven to 180°C. To make the pastry: Place flours and butter in a large bowl and rub with your fingers until it resembles breadcrumbs. Add water and mix with a butter knife until the pastry just comes together. Divide into 2 portions and roll each out to a 28 cm circle on a well-floured surface.

Line a lightly greased baking tin with one circle of pastry. Prick the base with a fork. Fill with quandong filling, and trim the edge of the pastry. Cut remaining pastry into smaller circles using a 7 cm round cutter.

Mix the egg and the cream together. Brush the edges of the pastry with mixture. Lay circles of pastry over the pie, overlapping slightly. Brush the top of the pie with the egg mixture. Sprinkle with sugar. Bake for 30–35 minutes, or until golden.

Serve with the native ice creams on page 219.

Candied Flowers

These make the perfect addition to any cake or are wonderful for a wedding bomboniere, hens' do or grown-up lolly bag. You can pretty much candy most edible petals and flowers – just play around with them until you find your favourites.

Prep Time: 10 minutes

2 handfuls of small or 1 handful of large edible flowers, e.g. sprigs of Geraldton wax, chocolate and vanilla lilies, banksia petals and parakeelya flowers
110–225 g caster sugar
3 free-range egg whites

Line 2 baking trays with baking paper and set aside.

Shake out any little critters from the petals and flowers. You can rinse them but will then need to wait until they are thoroughly dried before using. Cut the head of the large flowers from the stem. Carefully hold the base and pull off the petals from the centre and place aside.

Put the sugar in a small bowl. Lightly whisk the egg whites in another small bowl until frothy. Now get a production line going. Using a pastry brush, lightly brush each petal, front and back, with egg white. Dip into the sugar, evenly coating each side of the petal, then place onto the lined baking tray. Repeat with the remainder of the petals and flowers. Once they are all coated, leave them somewhere warm but not humid to dry overnight. They are ready when they are hard enough to eat like sweets.

Store in an airtight container for up to a week, taking care to keep the layers of petals and flowers separate with baking paper.

Fermented Flower Water

You can (much like our animal friends do) suck the nectar out of the flowers, or soak the flowers in water to make a sweet drink. Here's how you do it.

Prep Time: 5 minutes
Wait Time: up to one week

banksia or bottlebrush flowers

Note: The flowers come out in spring or mid-summer and it is best to pick them just before the birds get them, when they are filled with nectar... but remember to leave enough behind for regeneration and our wildlife. Bees, wasps and other insects suck the nectar from the banksia flowers, and honeyeater birds and possums like them, too.

Pick banksia flowers or bottlebrush which have lots of nectar. Shake out any critters and leave them in the garden, please! Give the flowers a rinse and shake off the excess water.

Place the flowers in a large bowl and cover with cold filtered water. Cover loosely with a clean tea towel. Leave in the fridge or a cool spot in the pantry for up to a week. The liquid will be ready when it tastes honey-flavoured. Drain the sweet water and drink. Or leave the flowers in the water for longer to ferment. When the mixture is slightly carbonated, strain the flowers and drink the liquid.

Illawarra Plum & Lemon Myrtle Limoncello Trifle

There are trifle lovers and trifle haters. I think it's the soggy biscuits that throw people into worlds of love or hate. Trifle is pretty Australian and always (if done well) a show-stopper. This recipe can be made in one large centrepiece dish or in small individual glasses.

Serves 6–8

Prep Time: 20 minutes

100 g ooray plums
300 g Illawarra plums
4 Victoria or red plums
100 ml orange juice
zest of 1 orange
2 tablespoons sugar
100 g native cherries
1 whole sponge cake or 1 packet sponge
  finger biscuits (savoiardi or ladyfingers)
180 ml boiling water
1 tablespoon ground lemon myrtle
150–200 ml limoncello or Green Ant
  Citronello (see page 88)
500 ml thickened cream
2 tablespoons icing sugar, sifted
1 teaspoon wattleseed extract (optional)
500 ml custard, homemade or bought

Note: This recipe can be made up to one full day before serving.

Halve the plums and discard the stones. The Illawarra plums have very small stones so just put them in whole. Put the plums into a small saucepan with the orange juice, zest and sugar, and bring to the boil. Reduce the heat and simmer gently until the plums are falling apart. Add the cherries right at the end to keep their texture. Leave to cool.

If using a sponge cake, cut it into 2 cm slices. Select a serving bowl and layer the cake slices or biscuits in the base and a little way up the sides.

Boil the water in a kettle, pour into a bowl and mix the hot water with the lemon myrtle powder until dissolved. Stir in the limoncello (add more or less limoncello directly to the sponge depending on how soggy you like the cake) and pour the mixture over the cake. Push the cake down to soak up the liquid.

Whip the cream with the sifted icing sugar (and wattleseed extract, if using) until thick. Swirl the custard through the cream mixture. To assemble the trifle, spoon the cooled plum mixture on top of the cake, then the custard mixture. Refrigerate for 30 minutes before serving.

Rosella Relish

While the rosella is not actually native to Australia (it's from Africa), it grows wild here and has adapted its own unique flavours in Australia. It is used by many in 'bush tucker' recipes and sold as a native flower; plus, it's bloody delightful. Use it with your Christmas ham or on a cheese board.

Makes 4 jars

Prep Time: 5 minutes
Cooking Time: 20 minutes

2 kg fresh rosella flowers
4–6 lemon myrtle leaves, whole
1 cup white sugar per 1 cup of pulp

Remove the petals from the seed pods (the hard green calyces) of the rosella flowers. Wash the petals and seed pods separately and shake off excess water.

Place the pods in a medium-sized heavy-based saucepan and cover with water. Boil over medium-high heat for 30 minutes.

Place the petals in another saucepan. When the pods have cooked, strain the juice directly over the petals in the other saucepan. Discard the pods.

Add the lemon myrtle leaves to the petals and bring slowly to the boil then continue to cook for about 20 minutes. Once the mixture reduces to pulp, remove from the heat. Measure the pulp, add sugar in equal proportion and stir to dissolve.

Bring the mix quickly back to the boil for 20 minutes, or until setting point is reached. Cool for a few minutes, remove lemon myrtle leaves then transfer to 4 x 500 ml jars. Store in a cool, dark place for up to 2 years.

Davidson's Plum Hot Chocolate

This is a great recipe and you can play around with different herbs and edible flowers. Try finger lime, anise myrtle, lemon myrtle, wattleseed and strawberry gum powders. Another alternative is to switch the dark chocolate for white – use half the amount, and no honey, as it is sweet in itself.

Serves 2

Prep Time: 5 minutes
Cooking Time: 5 minutes

250 ml full-cream milk
250 ml pouring cream
150 g dark chocolate (70% is best)
1–2 teaspoons Davidson's plum powder
1 tablespoon honey (optional)
extra whipped cream, to serve

Put all the ingredients into a small saucepan and heat slowly, stirring, until the chocolate melts completely. Don't let the milk boil. Serve in your favourite mugs.

Rainforest & Bush Fruit Sorbets

Sorbets are the perfect way to use native fruits as many of them are seasonal and you will have to purchase them frozen because of the supply and demand. To make the sorbet, purée the frozen fruit in a food processor or using a hand blender. These are some of my favourite combinations.

Serves 2

Prep Time: 5 minutes
Wait Time: 3 hours

250 g fruit, frozen, or – if fresh, peeled, de-stoned, chopped, and frozen
icing sugar or honey, to sweeten
spices or herbs, to taste
booze or juice, to taste

Mango, Blood Lime & Honey

Blend chunks of frozen mango with a dash of blood lime juice, pulp and zest and a little honey until smooth. Freeze for 30 minutes once puréed for a firmer texture.

Spiced Pear & Illawarra Plum

Blend frozen chunks of peeled and cored pears with a handful of Illawarra plums (without the seeds), a drizzle of maple syrup and a pinch of ground cinnamon myrtle, until smooth. Freeze for 30 minutes once puréed for a firmer texture.

Wild Raspberry & Rose

Blend frozen native raspberries with a few teaspoons of icing sugar, to taste, and 1 teaspoon rosewater or dried rose petals, until smooth. The berries will need a little extra blending as their texture isn't as smooth and creamy as soft fruits like pears, but keep blending and it'll get there. Freeze for 30 minutes once puréed for a firmer texture.

Bush Apple Pie

Use 2 bush apples and a handful of muntries per person. Remove the large seeds from the bush apple, slice and then refreeze if needed. Blend the apples, muntries, a few teaspoons of icing sugar, to taste, a large pinch of ground cinnamon myrtle and a large pinch of mixed spice, until smooth. Freeze for 30 minutes once puréed for a firmer texture.

Lemon Aspen & Boab Nut

Blend frozen lemon aspen with 1 teaspoon boab powder and a few teaspoons of honey, to taste, until smooth. Freeze for 30 minutes once puréed for a firmer texture.

Boonjie Tamarind & Coconut

Blend frozen tamarind with a few teaspoons of honey, to taste, and 2 tablespoons coconut cream until smooth. Freeze for 10–20 minutes once puréed for a firmer texture.

Pickled Lilly Pilly

You may never have noticed before but now that you are looking, it's pretty safe to say there is a lilly pilly tree near you. These pretty pink fruits are in jars filling my pantry.

Makes 4 jars

Prep Time: 10 minutes
Cooking Time: 10 minutes

700 ml apple cider vinegar
200 ml water
1 cup brown or white sugar
½ teaspoon ground lemon myrtle
½ teaspoon ground anise myrtle
¼ teaspoon ground cinnamon
8 cloves
8 cardamon pods, brusied
2 pinches of salt
1 kg lilly pillies (fresh is best)
2 cinnamon quills
bay leaves

Note: *Once open, the fruit will lose their colour in the jar.*

In a small saucepan, place all the ingredients except the lilly pillies, cinnamon quills and bay leaves. Bring to the boil, stirring the sugar until fully dissolved before the temperature gets too hot. Once boiling, reduce the heat and simmer for 15–20 minutes so the flavours can infuse.

Place the fruit into 4 x 250 ml sterilised jars, adding some cinnamon and bay leaves intermittently as decorations. Fill the jars with the hot pickling liquid, leaving about 1 cm head space, and seal.

Store in a cool, dark place for 1 or 2 months before eating, and up to 2 years. The longer the better. You can also store in the fridge.

Wild Shrubs

A shrub is a vinegar health drink. You can use these recipes as a base and experiment with any fruit you like. Let the shrub ferment, then, to drink, simply dilute a shot with some soda water, and sweetener should you need it. A perfect mocktail, a health shot, or add vodka for a fabulous cocktail.

Place all the ingredients into a sterilised jar, making sure you have enough vinegar to cover the fruit. Stir to dissolve the maple syrup or honey. Place the lid on, shake to mix, and store in a dry, cool place out of direct sunlight for at least a month. Shake every other day.

Lilly Pilly & Rose Shrub

250 g lilly pillies
270 ml apple cider vinegar
4 tablespoons maple syrup or raw honey
1 tablespoon dried rose petals

Rainforest Cherry & Hibiscus Shrub

250 g rainforest cherries
270 ml apple cider vinegar
1 rosella flower
4 tablespoons maple syrup or raw honey
1 teaspoon ground cinnamon myrtle
4–5 cloves

Boonjie Tamarind Shrub

250 g fresh boonjie tamarind
270 ml apple cider vinegar
2 sprigs of native thyme
6 tablespoons maple syrup or raw honey

Toffee Apple Shrub

250 g muntries and bush apples, muntries whole, bush apples halved and seeds removed
270 ml apple cider vinegar
5 tablespoons maple syrup
1 tablespoon raw honey
pinch of ground cinnamon myrtle

Leaves & Greens

It was a leaf that changed things for me – the lemon myrtle leaf. When I first tasted it, I had an 'aha!' moment, and a huge realisation that, while I am Australian, I had never eaten truly local food. That lemon myrtle leaf inspired me to learn more. Since then I have been more curious than ever, and even more determined to protect what there is still to learn.

Some of the trees in our backyard have very powerful leaves, not just medicinally but also in flavour. There are a number of properties that make our plants valuable in medicine, including tannins, mucilage, oils, latex, alkaloids and several other compounds. But we do have to be careful. For example, the leaves and bark of the eucalyptus are considered poisonous in large amounts. If too much is ingested, you can get food poisoning. With any native plant, unless you are 100 per cent certain of its toxicity level, do not eat it. Be especially cautious when out foraging and only pick things you have identified, and always leave enough behind for the wildlife and regeneration.

The leaves in this book are common varieties like lemon, cinnamon and anise myrtle, and a bunch of gums like strawberry and peppermint. There are so many more available in nature, but not yet available in stores. I hope in time that will change. For now, though, order a few of these online and have a play.

When it comes to the greens, your mind is about to get blown. Plants you have undoubtedly walked past many times at the beach or seen as groundcover, like karkalla or pig face, are delicious. Salty, crunchy and full of moisture. Same goes for that silvery plant that looks like rosemary. Yep, it's rosemary – the native kind. And those spinach-looking leaves – they're warrigal greens or native spinach. I hope that by sharing just a few of them in this book you'll be inspired to use them and even grow them in your own garden.

Strawberry Gum Truffles

These are delectable. Fresh cream truffles – they can be made with any native spice. Try making them plain inside and rolling in ground Davidson's plum or ground finger lime for a sweet and sour combination.

Makes 12

Prep Time: 10 minutes
Fridge Time: 1 hour

150 ml double cream
5 g dried strawberry gum leaves, crushed
125 g dark chocolate
1 tablespoon unsalted butter
pinch of sea salt
icing sugar or cocoa powder, to serve

Gently warm the cream in a saucepan and stir in the crushed dried strawberry gum leaves.

Finely chop the chocolate. Place in a heat-proof bowl that will sit nicely and snugly over the pan of gently warming cream. Once the cream is warmed through and the chocolate has just started to melt, take the saucepan off the heat. Let it sit for 10 minutes, allowing the cream to infuse with the strawberry gum flavours and the chocolate to continue to slowly melt.

Remove the chocolate from the cream pan – it's okay if it's not fully melted. Place the cream back over the heat just long enough to just warm it through. Strain the cream over the chocolate, discarding the strawberry gum leaves, but really squeeze the leaves from the cream to extract as much flavour as possible.

Add the butter and a pinch of salt to the chocolate mixture. Gently stir through to combine. You should get a glossy, silky mixture. If for some reason the mixture splits – meaning the fat separates from the cocoa solids (this is caused by overmixing or getting the chocolate too hot), *(continued over page)*

add 1 tablespoon of boiling water to the mixture and vigorously whisk or blend in a food processer until silky and smooth.

Chill in the fridge or freezer until set. Scoop up by the rounded teaspoon and coat in icing sugar or cocoa powder. If you have a coffee grinder you could even grind up some strawberry gum leaves with your cocoa powder or icing sugar for added flavour.

Store the truffles in the fridge until ready to serve. They will keep for a week in the fridge, or you can freeze them.

Sea Rosemary Poached Pears

These are best served with cream, custard, ice cream or all of the above. They're also great with crème fraîche or yoghurt. If you are vegan, try one of the wonderful sorbets from page 191.

Serves 4

Prep Time: 20 minutes
Cooking Time: 30 minutes

500 ml filtered water, wine or
    Applewood Red Okar
4 tablespoons raw honey
4–6 sprigs of sea rosemary
3 lemon myrtle leaves
3 anise myrtle leaves
3 strawberry gum leaves
1 teaspoon cloves
1 teaspoon pepperberries, crushed
4 pears (Conference or Bosc), peeled,
    cored and quartered (you can leave
    the peel on if you wish)
juice of ½ lemon

In a large saucepan, place the water or wine and honey over medium heat and stir until the honey is dissolved. Add all the aromatics.

Place the pears in the saucepan and cover with a circle of baking paper with a small hole cut in the middle. Bring the liquid to a low boil and simmer the pears for 20–25 minutes, depending on the texture you like.

Once cooked, add the lemon juice and leave the pears to sit in their liquid for about 20 minutes before serving. You can also put the pears into sterilised jars and then top with the liquid and store in a cool, dark place for up to a year, or keep in an airtight container in the fridge for a week.

Beetroot, Ginger & Anise Myrtle Soup

This soup is not just delicious, it's also wonderful when you are feeling a little run-down. Like a big licoricy hug. Anise myrtle and beetroot go beautifully together. If you don't like licorice, use ground lemon myrtle leaves in the same quantity as the anise myrtle.

Serves 6

Prep Time: 10 minutes
Cooking Time: 10 minutes

600 g beetroot
1 small brown onion
1 garlic clove
1 green apple, peeled
drizzle of olive or nut oil
1 tablespoon ground anise myrtle
25 g fresh ginger, grated
500 ml chicken or vegetable stock
salt and pepper, to taste
yoghurt, for garnish

Top and tail the beetroots, but don't peel them; you want to keep the nutrients in the peel. Cut them into quarters, place in a saucepan and cover with water. Bring to the boil and cook until tender. This can take up to 40 minutes.

Finely chop the onion, garlic and apple. Cook the onion, garlic, apple, anise myrtle and ginger in a saucepan with a drizzle of oil over low–medium heat, stirring occasionally, until soft and almost transparent. Add the stock and cook for a few minutes.

Once the beetroot is tender, place into a blender with the stock mixture and blend until smooth, or leave it a bit chunkier if you prefer. You may need to do this in smaller batches.

Add salt and pepper to taste, and serve with a dollop of yoghurt. You can reheat the soup, or serve it cold.

Sea Rosemary, Lime & Murray River Salt Anzac Biscuits

This recipe is both sweet and savoury. Make the biscuits flat
and thin and use them with cheese as a gorgeous
alternative to crackers.

Makes 12

Prep Time: 10 minutes
Cooking Time: 20 minutes

1¼ cups plain flour, sifted
1 teaspoon ground cinnamon myrtle
1 cup rolled oats
¾ cup shredded coconut
¼ cup caster sugar
zest of 4 blood limes
2 long sprigs of sea rosemary, coarsely
  chopped, stems removed and
  discarded
½ teaspoon Murray River pink salt, plus
  extra for sprinkling
1 tablespoon golden syrup or treacle
1 tablespoon honey
150 g unsalted butter, chopped
½ teaspoon bicarbonate of soda
1½ tablespoons water

Preheat the oven to 185°C. Line 2 baking trays with
baking paper.

In a large bowl, place the flour, cinnamon myrtle, oats,
coconut, sugar, lime zest, sea rosemary and salt, and
stir to combine.

In a small saucepan, place the golden syrup, honey and
butter and stir over low heat until the butter has melted.
Remove from the heat. Mix the bicarbonate of soda
with the water and add to the golden syrup mixture.
Pour into the dry ingredients and mix together until fully
combined.

Roll tablespoonfuls of the mixture into balls and place
on baking trays, pressing down on the top to flatten.
Sprinkle with a little salt, to taste.

Bake for 12–20 minutes until golden brown, depending
on the thickness of your biscuit.

Lemon Myrtle Pasta

Homemade pasta is absolutely the best. You can vary this lemon
myrtle pasta by switching out the lemon myrtle with 1 tablespoon
of ground wattleseed, or even make pepperberry pasta using
½ tablespoon of ground pepperberry.

Serves 4–6

Prep Time: 30 minutes
Cooking Time: 5 minutes

140 g good-quality plain flour
1 tablespoon ground lemon myrtle
140 g hard wheat semolina
2 large free-range eggs
pinch of salt

In a large bowl, mix the flour, lemon myrtle and
semolina with your hands. Make a well in the centre
and crack in the eggs, then add the salt. Mix to a dough
then turn out onto a floured surface. Knead for up to
5 minutes, or until smooth. If the dough feels too dry
while kneading, add a few drops of water as necessary.
If too wet, add a little more flour. Cover the dough with a
tea towel and leave to rest for 1 hour.

If you have a pasta machine, follow the instructions to
make tagliatelle. If not, use a rolling pin to roll the dough
into very thin sheets and cut into strips 1 cm wide and
about 20 cm long.

Cook in boiling salted water for a few minutes, or
until al dente.

Strawberry Gum Pavlova

Many Australians would argue (with New Zealanders!) that there is nothing more Australian than a pavlova. I would argue there is, and it's this one.

Serves 8

Prep Time: 15 minutes
Cooking Time: 1.5 hours

9 free-range egg whites
3 teaspoons boiling water
3 tablespoons ground strawberry gum
300 g caster sugar
1 teaspoon white vinegar

For the lemon myrtle cream:
300 ml cream
60 g icing sugar, sifted
1 teaspoon lemon myrtle extract

100 g rosella, riberries, muntries
edible flowers, to decorate

Place a large bowl, 20–25 cm diameter, on baking paper and trace around it to draw a circle. Turn the paper upside down on a baking tray so you can see the circle outline.

To make the meringue: Place all the ingredients into a stand mixer bowl and, using the whisk attachment, beat on high for 10 minutes. Pile the meringue into the circle on the baking paper and use a spatula to spread evenly to the edges. If you like, you can use an upward motion with a palette knife to decorate the edges. Try to get a smooth top to make filling with the cream easier. Rough and rustic is also fine.

Preheat the oven to 100°C. Bake the meringue for 1½ hours. Turn the tray halfway through the cooking time. When cooked, turn off the oven and let the meringue cool completely in the oven before removing. If not serving within a few hours, wrap in plastic wrap or store in an airtight container for up to 3 days.

To make the lemon myrtle cream: In a bowl, whip the cream with the icing sugar and lemon myrtle extract.

Pile the cream evenly on the meringue base and decorate with the berries and flowers.

Fermented Greens

We love anything fermented. It's a fabulously healthy product but also helps to extend the shelf life of foods. Add your fermented greens to salads, sandwiches and soups.

Makes 1 jar

Prep Time: 5 minutes
Wait Time: 2 weeks

250 g karkalla and/or samphire
1 garlic clove
1 red chilli
6 per cent salt brine

Make a 6 per cent salt brine solution with filtered water. Mix a ratio of 6 per cent salt to 1 litre of water until dissolved.

Pack a 250 ml jar with all ingredients. Cover with salt brine.

Leave to ferment for 1–2 weeks out of direct sunlight.

'Burp' your jar a few times in the first week by simply twisting the lid to allow carbon dioxide to escape but don't let oxygen into the jar.

Pickled Greens

A wonderful addition to any salad, in toasties or a topping for barbecued meats, or eaten straight from the jar.

Makes 2 jars

Prep Time: 10 minutes
Cooking Time: 20 minutes

500 g greens (karkalla and/or samphire)
extra garnish, such as chilli, lemon myrtle or aniseed myrtle leaves, or whole pepperberries
120 g sugar
250 ml apple cider vinegar
75 ml water
125 ml white wine vinegar
1 teaspoon ground lemon myrtle or leaves
1 teaspoon pepperberries, crushed
½ teaspoon salt
pinch of chilli flakes
extra salt, to taste

Note: This recipe also makes a great quick pickle. Use the same method but leave in a bowl to pickle for an hour before eating. You can store any leftovers in a container in the fridge for up to a week.

Pack 2 x 250 ml jars with greens. Add any extra garnish to jars, such as chilli, lemon myrtle or aniseed myrtle leaves, or whole pepperberries.

Into a medium saucepan, add all remaining ingredients, heat on low and stir until sugar is dissolved. Heat to high and simmer for 20 minutes to infuse flavours. Strain and pour the hot liquid into the jars. Seal and store in a cool, dark place for 1 month before eating.

Rainforest Marshmallows

You can choose your own adventure here – strawberry gum, peppermint gum, lemon myrtle, cinnamon myrtle or anise myrtle (all available in ground form). These marshmallows are best toasted and sprinkled with a little Murray River sea salt, eaten straight after toasting on the fire.

Makes 8–10

Prep Time: 10 minutes
Cooking Time: 1 hour

olive oil spray, for greasing
4½ teaspoons powdered gelatine
180 ml water
165 g caster sugar
125 ml glucose syrup
¼ teaspoon Murray River pink salt
1 tablespoon ground strawberry gum or any ground native leaf
extra Murray River pink salt, for garnish

Note: *Thread onto eucalypt sticks before toasting on the fire.*

Lightly coat a 21 cm x 11 cm shallow baking tin with olive oil spray.

In a small bowl, whisk together the gelatine and 60 ml of the water, then leave it to sit for 5 minutes.

Place the sugar, 60 ml of the glucose, the salt and the remaining water in a medium-sized saucepan over high heat. Bring to the boil, then continue boiling rapidly, stirring occasionally, until the temperature reaches 115°C on a probe thermometer.

Put the remaining glucose into the bowl of a stand mixer fitted with the whisk attachment. Microwave the gelatine mix on high until melted, about 30 seconds, stirring once or twice. Pour into the stand mixer bowl, then turn the mixer on to low and keep it running.

Once the sugar syrup reaches 115°C, remove from the heat and slowly pour it into the mixer bowl, whisking continuously. Increase the speed to medium and whisk for a further 5 minutes. Increase the speed to medium-high and whisk for another 5 minutes.
(continued over page)

Add the strawberry gum, then increase to the highest speed and whisk until fluffy.

Pour the marshmallow mix into the greased baking tin, banging the tray on the benchtop to spread evenly and smoothing the surface with a palette knife. Leave in a cool, dry place for about 6 hours to set.

Line a second baking tray with baking paper. Cut the set marshmallow slab into rectangles using a knife or pizza cutter, then transfer to the tray.

Thread onto sticks, toast, sprinkle with salt and enjoy!

Native Leaf Ice Creams

This is the purest form of ice cream and the joy of it is that you don't need an ice-cream maker, nor do you need to churn it in any way. Just make and freeze.

Serves 2

Prep Time: 5 minutes
Wait Time: 2 hours

choose your leaf and use in ground form:
    strawberry gum – 1–2 teaspoons
    (the latter for stronger flavour)
    peppermint gum & choc chip – 1
      teaspoon and 1 tablespoon
    licorice (anise myrtle) – 1 teaspoon
    lemon myrtle – 1 teaspoon
250 ml single or double cream
3 tablespoons runny honey
3 egg yolks
seeds scraped from ½ vanilla pod or
    1 teaspoon vanilla extract

Heat the cream with your choice of native leaf for about 5 minutes until warm (not boiling). Remove from the heat and leave to steep in the fridge for as long as you can; overnight is best. Sieve the cream before using again.

Heat the honey in a cup in the microwave until just warmed. Put the egg yolks in a medium-sized bowl and whisk in the warm honey. Add the cream and the vanilla and whip for a couple of minutes. Stir through choc chips, if using. Pour into a freezer-proof dish. Cover and freeze for 2–3 hours, or until firm.

Saltbush & Muntrie Soda Bread

We love soda bread. It is really very easy to make. Don't be put off thinking bread is hard and laborious to make, this one is not at all. The salty saltbush makes it so darn good hot out of the oven with lashings of butter. You could use bush tomato or wattleseed, too.

Serves 6–8

Prep Time: 10 minutes
Cooking Time: 45 minutes

340 g wholemeal self-raising flour
340 g plain flour
3 teaspoon ground saltbush
1 teaspoon bicarbonate of soda
small pinch of salt
580 ml buttermilk
⅔ cup muntries
drizzle of olive oil
2 tablespoons saltbush seeds, for topping
2 sprigs of sea rosemary, finely chopped
extra muntries, for garnish and to serve

Preheat the oven to 200°C.

Put the flours, saltbush, bicarbonate of soda and pinch of salt into a large mixing bowl and stir. Make a well in the middle and pour in the buttermilk and muntries. Mix quickly with a fork to form a soft dough. Add more buttermilk if it's too dry and more flour if too sticky.

Turn out onto a floured surface and knead briefly (don't overknead or it will be hard as a rock). Shape it into a 30 cm loaf, flatten slightly and place onto a baking tray lined with baking paper. Cut a cross in the top of the loaf, lightly brush on some oil and sprinkle with the saltbush seeds and sea rosemary. Bake for about 45 minutes, or until the loaf sounds hollow when you knock the bottom.

Wild Basil & Bush Tomato Gazpacho

Wild basil is super. It's much stronger than the stuff we are used to. It's also pretty easy to grow in a pot on your balcony or in your garden. This soup can be served hot or chilled in summer.

Serves 2–4

Prep Time: 10 minutes
Cooking Time: 30 minutes

2 tablespoons lemon myrtle infused
   olive oil
1 onion, chopped
2 garlic cloves, crushed
½ teaspoon pepperberries, crushed
3 tablespoons ground bush tomato,
   plus extra for sprinkling
12 ripe tomatoes, chopped
1 tablespoon sugar
1 cup chicken or vegetable stock
1 bunch of wild basil, chopped, with a
   few leaves reserved for garnish
salt and freshly ground pepperberry
crème fraîche, to serve

Note: This soup can be made and stored frozen when you have a glut of tomatoes in summer and stocked up to eat hot in winter.

Heat the oil in a large saucepan over medium heat and sauté the onion and garlic until the onion is softened. Add the pepperberries, bush tomato, chopped tomato and sugar, and simmer for 30 minutes. The tomatoes will break down. Add the stock and bring to the boil.

Take off the heat, add the basil and season with salt and pepperberry to taste. Using a hand-held blender, purée until the tomato skins are incorporated.

Serve sprinkled with ground bush tomato, with a dollop of crème fraîche and a garnish of wild basil.

Salt & Vinegar Crisps

These are simply ace. A little like kale crisps but with more texture. Try this recipe with any edible native leaves, and different kinds of salt and spice combinations.

Serves 1

Prep Time: 2 minutes
Cooking Time: 10 minutes

10 ml apple cider vinegar
large pinch of sea salt
2 handfuls of saltbush leaves
chilli flakes or ground pepperberry leaf,
  to taste
spray bottle

Preheat the oven to 160°C. Line a baking tray with baking paper.

Place the vinegar and salt in a spray bottle and shake to combine, then spray the saltbush leaves lightly all over.

Spread the leaves out on the baking tray in a single layer. Sprinkle with chilli or ground pepperberry. Bake for about 10 minutes, or until crisp. Remove from the oven and leave to cool completely on the baking tray. Store in an airtight container – they will keep for a few days.

Green Gnocchi with Cinnamon Myrtle Burnt Butter Sauce

Stop drooling.

Serves 2

Prep Time: 10 minutes
Cooking Time: 5 minutes

400 g warrigal greens
handful of sea parsley, finely chopped
1 garlic clove, crushed
140 g ricotta
85 g plain flour
2 free-range eggs
100 g grated Parmesan cheese
salt and pepper, to taste

For the burnt butter sauce:
100 g butter
1 teaspoon ground cinnamon myrtle,
  plus extra to sprinkle
1 garlic clove

1 sprig of sea parsley, leaves picked, to
  garnish
salt and pepper, to taste

Place 300 g of the warrigal greens in a bowl and pour boiling water over them. Leave for 1–2 minutes until wilted, drain thoroughly, squeeze out excess water and finely chop.

Place the warrigal greens, parsley, garlic, ricotta, flour, eggs and cheese in a large bowl and season with salt and pepper. Use a fork to stir very thoroughly.

On a floured surface, roll the dough into finger-sized lengths then cut into 3 cm portions. Place on baking tray lined with baking paper and refrigerate for at least 30 minutes before cooking.

Boil a large pot of salted water and cook the gnocchi until just cooked, a few minutes. They will float to the top when cooked. Drain and set aside.

To make the burnt butter sauce: In a large saucepan over medium heat, melt the butter with the cinnamon myrtle, garlic and remaining warrigal greens. Cook for 5–6 minutes, or until the butter is slightly brown.

Toss the gnocchi through the sauce, stir through the sea parsley leaves and season with salt and pepper to taste. Sprinkle with cinnamon myrtle to serve.

Bunya Nut Pesto

Just about every cookbook has a pesto recipe, I know. But I can actually say this one is different, because it is!

Makes 350 grams

Prep Time: 10 minutes

250 g warrigal greens
3 finger limes, caviar only
1 cup macadamia oil
50 g sea parsley, finely chopped
50 g wild basil, finely chopped
10 desert limes
100 g macadamias, toasted and
  chopped
100 g bunya nuts, toasted and chopped
3 garlic cloves
juice of 2 lemons
salt and ground pepperberry, to taste
70 g grated Parmesan cheese

Blanch the warrigal greens in boiling water for 1 minute then refresh in cold water. Drain well and roughly chop.

Place the greens in a food processor with the finger lime caviar and a drizzle of macadamia oil, and blitz until a purée begins. Add the parsley, basil, desert limes, macadamias, bunya nuts and garlic and continue to blitz, drizzling in the remaining oil slowly. Add lemon juice and give one more blitz.

Remove from the food processor into a bowl and season with salt and pepperberry to taste. Mix through the Parmesan and adjust seasonings if needed. Store in a sterilised jar in the fridge.

Warrigal Greens, Coconut & Egg Rice

This is a perfect mid-week feed. You can also make extra for lunches and breakfasts. Keep in an airtight container and reheat as necessary. Use an emu egg instead of hen's eggs.

Serves 1–2

Prep Time: 5 minutes
Cooking Time: 5 minutes

½ cup wild rice
1 teaspoon coconut oil
3 free-range eggs
drizzle of olive oil
1 chilli, finely chopped
½ teaspoon grated turmeric
1 garlic clove, finely chopped
3 kale leaves, chopped
large handful of warrigal greens
¼ cup frozen baby peas, defrosted
juice of 1 lemon, to serve
salt and ground pepperberry, to taste
2 tablespoons Woodside lemon myrtle
   goat's cheese or natural yoghurt,
   to serve

Cook the wild rice, drain and set aside.

In a large frypan over medium heat, add the coconut oil and let it melt, then crack the eggs and quickly scramble. Remove and set aside.

In the same pan over low heat, add a little olive oil and cook the chilli, turmeric and garlic for 1 minute. Add the kale, warrigal greens and peas. Cook for 1 minute, or until the greens are wilted, then add the rice and egg to the pan.

Season to taste with salt and pepperberry, heat through and serve with lemon juice and goat's cheese scattered on top.

Crispy-fried Saltbush Trees

Such a fabulous appetiser or snack with a glass of fino sherry
or Okar! Keep the saltbush in 10 cm stalks with the leaves to make
for easy eating while standing.

Serves 10 as a snack

Prep Time: 5 minutes
Cooking Time: 10 minutes

For the batter:
55 g rice flour
55 g plain flour
½ teaspoon baking powder
pinch of salt
1 free-range egg
300 ml soda water, chilled

vegetable oil, for deep-frying
10–15 saltbush stems with leaves

To make the batter: Place all the ingredients in a
large bowl and mix with a whisk until combined. It is
important not to overmix and don't worry if it's not super
smooth. Set aside.

Pour enough vegetable oil into a deep saucepan to
one-third full. Heat over a medium-high heat until a little
drop of batter sizzles immediately when dropped in.

Dip the saltbush stems into the batter to coat, and
shake off any excess. Holding the stem with tongs,
place the saltbush into the hot oil and deep-fry for 1–2
minutes, or until golden brown. They are really delicate
so you don't need to cook them for long. Don't overcrowd
the pan; only deep-fry a few stems at a time.

Once cooked, remove the stems using a slotted spoon
and place on paper towel to remove excess oil.

Wattleseed, Wild Basil & River Mint Berries

This is simply the easiest dinner-party dazzler you will ever make.
The further in advance you make it, the better it tastes.

Serves 2–4

Prep Time: 5 minutes
Wait Time: 2 hours

375 g strawberries or native raspberries
½ cup muntries
¼ cup coconut sugar or brown sugar
2 lemons, zest of 1, juice of both
large handful of native basil,
   leaves picked
small handful of river mint,
   leaves picked
2 tablespoons wattleseed balsamic
   vinegar
ground pepperberry, to taste

Wash, pat dry, hull and quarter the strawberries or native raspberries. You can leave them halved if you prefer. Place in a large bowl with the muntries and mix in the sugar, adding more or less sugar to your taste. Zest 1 of the lemons and add the zest to the bowl, then add the juice of both lemons; use less zest or juice if you prefer. Add the basil leaves, mint leaves, wattleseed balsamic, and pepperberry and mix it all together.

Put in the fridge until dessert time or for at least an hour. The longer you leave it, the more it will be infused with the herbs.

Our Everyday Health Drink

I have always been a big lemon-in-hot-water drinker. As a way to get as many beneficial herbs and spices into my diet (as we are not snackers), I put these beauties in a mug and keep it topped up with hot water all day long.

Makes 2 mugs

Prep Time: 5 minutes

5 Kakadu plums (cut a split in them)
3 cm piece of turmeric
3 cm piece of ginger
1 sprig of sea rosemary
5–6 desert limes, sliced and squeezed
1 lemon myrtle leaf
1 sprig of Geraldton wax
1 teaspoon raw local honey (optional)
lemon juice (optional)

Note: *The herbs and spices can be kept going for a couple of days before discarding and starting again.*

Place all the ingredients into 2 mugs and top with boiling water. Keep topping up with boiling water as you need to.

I would recommend adding a squeeze of lemon every few mugs.

DIY Native Tea Guide

Given that teas are our thing at Warndu, we wanted to share some of our favourite ingredients to make some pretty ace herbal teas. All of these ingredients have such incredible health benefits and are really easy to get your hands on in the dried form.

To make, blend your desired spice/herb or multiple, put a teaspoonful into a strainer/infuser and brew in a cup of nearly boiling water for 2–5 minutes, depending on the strength of your blend. A little experimenting is useful here.

Note: We would always suggest using dried ingredients for tea if you are going to store them or give them as gifts.

You can use fresh if you are drinking immediately and have access to these ingredients fresh.

Anise myrtle

Aroma of aniseed, menthol and herbs. Has outstanding antioxidant activity, as well as containing lutein, folate, vitamin E and vitamin C. Amazing blended with quandong as a digestif.

Bush tomato

Savoury caramelised aroma of carob; some cereal notes. Bush tomato has superior antioxidant capacity compared to the blueberry, which is renowned worldwide as a health-promoting fruit.

Davidson's plum

Aroma of rosella jam and stewed rhubarb; some musk and lolly notes. A good source of potassium and also contains lutein (a compound that plays an important role in eye health and wellbeing), vitamin E, folate, zinc, magnesium and calcium. Perfect with anything lemon.

Finger lime

Aroma of fresh zesty citrus with a hint of cooked citrus. High source of vitamins C, E, K, folate and potassium. Refreshing in the afternoon and great mixed with mint.

Kakadu plum

Aroma of stewed apples and pears; some cooked citrus, pickled and fermented notes. They don't just contain vitamin C, but additional lesser-known antioxidants like gallic acid (good for restoring the skin's natural barrier) and ellagic acid (helps restore elasticity to skin).

Lemon aspen

A fresh citrus aroma, conifer leaf and some chemical notes. A rich source of folate, iron and zinc; also contains magnesium and calcium. Use leaves or fruit.

Lemon myrtle

A lemon lolly aroma, perfumed with some menthol notes. It is a powerful antioxidant that can ward off illnesses, and it can be used as an antiseptic.

Lemon-scented gum

The leaves are packed with essential oils which are a powerful antiseptic and useful in helping fight colds and flu. Use sparingly. It is invigorating and energising.

Muntries

Aroma of moist fruit mince, spice, bush honey and butter. Like the acai berry is to the Amazon region, the muntrie appears to be a native superfood. A recent study of twelve native Australian fruits, the muntrie included, showed that the antioxidant capacity of many of these fruits were significantly higher than that of the blueberry, which is renowned for its high antioxidant levels.

Native lemongrass

Beautiful lemon sherbet aroma and subtle grassy flavour when heated. Great for sores, cramps and headaches. Excellent blended with lemon myrtle and lemon verbena.

Native thyme

Herbal aroma, bush shrub and menthol. A great palate cleanser, and promotes digestion. Freshly crushed leaves help with nausea and headache. Blend with rosemary for a savoury tea.

DIY Native Tea Guide
(continued)

Pepperberry

Aroma of bush shrub with perfumed, fruity, lolly notes. Lingering heat on the palate. Excellent with turmeric and has lots of antioxidants.

Pepperleaf

Aroma of Australian bushland, dry paperbark and herbs. Developing heat on the palate. Excellent with turmeric and has lots of antioxidants.

Quandong

Aroma of dry lentils; some earthy and fermented notes. Tastes like sour peach and dried sour fruit. Great sour profile in tea. Has twice the vitamin C of an orange, and is high in iron and zinc.

Riberry

A sweet, spiced tea aroma with musk, bush honey and resinous notes. Thought to assist in preventing or delaying conditions such as Alzheimer's disease, autoimmune and cardiovascular disease, cancer and diabetes. Riberry samples have also exhibited high levels of folate, otherwise known as vitamin B12.

River mint

Intense mint. More like spearmint than traditional mint. Great for digestion after dinner and for healing mouth infections. Can be made into a mouthwash by making a strong cup of tea and cooling it down before use.

Strawberry gum

My favourite of all the native spices. Smells like dried strawberry and is perfect in just about anything you would use strawberry for. Great for insomnia.
Note: Don't consume too much at a time. Like all eucalyptus, it should only be consumed in small doses.

Wattleseed

Aroma of toasted coffee grounds, sweet spice, raisin and chocolate. A caffeine-free pick-me-up.

Ingredients Index

*Comparisons is a handy shorthand reference to the flavour profile of the ingredient. There are no direct substitutions or comparisons.

COMMON NAME	SCIENTIFIC OR LATIN NAME	SEASONALITY	COMPARISONS*
Anise myrtle	*Syzygium anisatum*	Dried all year	Fennel, liquorice root
Banksia	*Banksia spp.*	Spring	—
Barilla spinach	*Tetragonia implexicoma*	All year fresh	English spinach
Blood lime	*Citrus australasica*	All year frozen	Tahitian lime
Bloodroot	*Haemodorum spicatum*	Rare	Curry leaves, capsicums, chilli
Boab	*Adansonia gregorii*	All year powdered	Chalky sherbet
Boobialla / Native juniper	*Myoporum insulare*	All year frozen	Juniper berries
Boonjie tamarind	*Diploglottis bracteata*	All year frozen	Rhubarb or under-ripe peaches
Bunya pine	*Araucaria bidwillii*	All year frozen	Pine nuts
Bush / lady / white apple	*Syzygium forte*	All year frozen	Granny Smith apples
Bush tomato, kutjera, or desert raisin	*Solanum centrale*	All year dried	Caramelised Vegemite, raisins
Chocolate lily & Vanilla lily	*Anthropodium strictum; Anthropodium milleflorum*	Rare	Chocolate/caramel & vanilla notes
Cinnamon myrtle	*Backhousia myrtifolia*	All year dried	Cinnamon
Davidson's plum	*Davidsonia jerseyana*	All year frozen	Tart and sour plum
Desert lime	*Citrus glauca*	All year frozen	Tahitian lime

COMMON NAME	SCIENTIFIC OR LATIN NAME	SEASONALITY	COMPARISONS*
Finger lime	*Citrus australasica*	All year frozen	Tahitian lime
Fish rushes	*Ficinia nodosa*	All year wholesale	Used for smoking foods
Geraldton wax	*Chamelaucium uncinatum*	All year fresh	Lemony pine needle
Green ants	*Oecophylla smaragdina*	All year frozen	Coriander seed and citrus
Illawarra plum	*Podocarpus elatus*	All year frozen	Tart and sour plum
Island celery	*Apium insulare*	Infrequent	Celery leaves
Kakadu plum	*Terminalia ferdinandiana*	All year dried and frozen	Vitamin C, sour and tart
Karkalla or Pig face	*Dishphyma crassifolium*	All year fresh	Salty and juicy bitter greens (bok choy in texture) but saltier
Lemon aspen	*Acronychia acidula*	All year frozen	Lemony apple
Lemon myrtle	*Backhousia citriodora*	All year dried	Lemon
Lemon-scented gum	*Corymbia citriodora*	All year dried	Lemon
Lilly pilly	*Syzygium spp.*	All year frozen	Clove/apple
Macadamia	*Macadamia integrifolia*	All year fresh	—
Makaya / bush pear	*Marsdenia australis*	Rare	Nashi pear
Minra / bullock bush	*Alectryon oleifolius*	Rare	Orange and carob

Ingredients Index (continued)

COMMON NAME	SCIENTIFIC OR LATIN NAME	SEASONALITY	COMPARISONS*
Muntries or Native apple	*Kunzea pomifera*	Feb–Mar fresh, or all year frozen	Granny Smith apple; hint of clove and sweetness
Murnong or Yam daisy	*Microseris lanceolata*	Rare	Potato
Native cherry or Cherry Ballart	*Exocarpos cupressiformis*	All year frozen	Tart cherries
Native currant	*Canthium latifolium*	All year frozen	Fresh currants but tart
Native curry bush	*Cassinia laevis*	Rare	Curry leaves
Native lemongrass	*Cymbopogon ambiguus*	All year dried	Lemongrass
Native orange	*Capparis mitchellii*	Rare	Passionfruit
Native raspberry	*Rubus probus*	Rare	Tart raspberries
Native thyme	*Prostanthera incisa*	All year dried	Thyme and mint
Ooray plum	*Davidsonia pruriens*	All year frozen	Tart and sour plum
Pandanus	*Pandanus spp.*	Rare	Coconut / walnuts
Parakeelya	*Calandrinia balonensis*	Rare	Cucumber
Pepperberry	*Tasmannia lanceolata*	All year dried	Aromatic pepper
Quandong or Urti	*Santalum acuminatum*	All year frozen	Sour peach
Rainforest cherry	*Syzygium aqueum*	All year frozen	Sour cherry

COMMON NAME	SCIENTIFIC OR LATIN NAME	SEASONALITY	COMPARISONS*
Riberry	*Syzygium luehmannii*	All year frozen and dried	Spicy, cloves and cinnamon berry
River mint	*Mentha australis*	All year dried	Spearmint/peppermint
Rosella	*Hibiscus sabdariffa*	All year frozen	Cranberry
Saltbush	*Atriplex spp.*	All year fresh	Salty and a crunchy seed
Samphire	*Tecticornia spp.*	All year fresh	Crisp, juicy, and salty
Sandalwood nut	*Santalum spicatum*	All year dried	Rice puffs
Seablite	*Suaeda australis*	All year fresh	Crisp, juicy and salty
Sea parsley	*Apium prostratum*	All year fresh	Parsley
Sea rosemary	*Olearia axillaris*	All year fresh	Rosemary
Strawberry gum	*Eucalyptus olida*	All year dried	Strawberries and cream aroma
Sunrise lime	*Citrus australasica*	All year frozen	Tahitian lime or kaffir lime leaves
Warrigal greens	*Tetragonia tetragonioides*	All year fresh	Spinach
Wattleseed	*Acacia victoriae*	All year dried	Coffee beans, Chocolate and coffee aroma and taste
Wild basil	*Ocimum tenuiflorum*	Spring–autumn fresh, all year dried	Holy basil
Youlk	*Platysace deflexa*	Rare	Radish/raw potato

Index

Acknowledgements

To our parents, Elson and Sunny Coulthard and Mandy and Andrew Sullivan. Without them we would never have come on this journey. You are undoubtedly our inspiration and support, always, along with our brothers and sisters, aunties, uncles and cousins aplenty. To the extended Coulthard family and Nepabunna community who have shared everything with us from Adnyamathanha words to uses of ingredients, and who have taken us foraging or shared valuable knowledge with us, thank you. In particular (aside from our parents and grandparents, of course), Gladys Wilton, Mick Coulthard, Noel Wilton, Granny Margaret Brown, Clifford Coulthard and Fanny Coulthard.

Our industry is brimming with amazing people doing incredible things. Some have been in this industry longer than we have walked the earth and to them, we owe immense gratitude. To those newbies, like us, collaboration is the key to longevity and sustainability for us all. The extended Australian native food industry – a huge, giant thank you to you all. You are a big bunch of small and large businesses and leaders, too many to thank on these pages. Chefs, farmers, growers, harvesters, value-adders, politicians, writers, activists (all listed in our online resource guide). So don't just gaze at this guide at www.warndu.com, pick up the phone, introduce yourself to someone and help each other out.

Bruce Pascoe, Dale Tilbrook and Ben Shewry – thanks for your inspired words. Bruce, your words in *Dark Emu* changed our trajectory in this industry for the better and we thank you for everything you do. Amanda Garner and Marianne Stewart, the ladies who invited me on to Australian Native Food and Botanicals as a board director and have literally put years of work behind the scenes into this industry and taught me so much. Also thank you to everyone else on the board: Russell and co for teaching me aplenty. Neville Bonney, thanks for being the greatest wealth of knowledge about these amazing ingredients and their botanical names; my true edit eyes. Gayle and Mike Quarmby, always generous with their fantastic produce and love for this industry.

Something Wild for the things you have shared with us for this shoot and during our many events for Warndu. Shannon Fleming for his advice in the early days of the book planning. Paul Iskov and Fervor, for having our backs and always inspiring us to do better. John Carty and Lara Torr at the South Australian Museum for letting us share Warndu with such a large bunch of people. Macro Meats, for always sharing the K-Roo love with us and supporting Warndu in so many ways. West Winds, Applewood Distillery and OKAR, thanks for that amazing Aussie booze to create fab cocktails with. Shezza at Finger Lime Caviar and Geraldine at Rainforest Bounty for the stunning rainforest fruits and Rebecca Barnes for my emergency delivery of the only ten fresh native raspberries you had and Geoff Woodall for the most perfect last-minute youlk a girl could ever ask for. To Kinfolk and Co for your stunning props and Lisa at Leap and Wander who made 90 per cent of all the incredible pottery on all the pages in this book. Her work was Warndu through and through and we love it and her!

Robert and Hachette. Thank you from the bottom of our hearts for taking on what other publishers called too 'niche' a topic and making a beautiful book with us. And who can forget the A team that made this book. Luisa Brimble on the lens who said yes to this project immediately and her enthusiasm at every tasting made us realise what we are doing is super-important. Shut the front door, Luisa! To Jess and Steve from Sage Creative, their work is the best in the business and their drinking and interpretive dance moves every night made shooting this book more fun than should have been allowed. Love you guys up to the Alkina (moon) and down to the Yarta (land). Ngaio Parr, your design of this book, bloody epic. Karen Ward, editor extraordinaire.

Last but not at all least. For those of you amazing home cooks who bought our book and are now using these beautiful ingredients, there are many people here for you to buy from and support! Thank you for growing this vital industry with us and more importantly, enjoy the journey, just like we are.

To our elders. Our grandparents. The love, knowledge and stories that
you shared have made us who we are today

◻ hachette
AUSTRALIA

Published in Australia and New Zealand in 2019
by Hachette Australia
(an imprint of Hachette Australia Pty Limited)
Level 17, 207 Kent Street, Sydney NSW 2000
www.hachette.com.au

10 9 8 7 6 5 4 3 2 1

A catalogue record for this
book is available from the
NATIONAL National Library of Australia
LIBRARY
OF AUSTRALIA

ISBN: 978 0 7336 4142 8 (hardback)

Cover and internal design by Ngaio Parr
Photography by Luisa Brimble
Food prep and styling by Sage Creative Co.
Endpapers and cover paintings by Damien Coulthard
Colour reproduction by Splitting Image
Printed in China by 1010 Printing

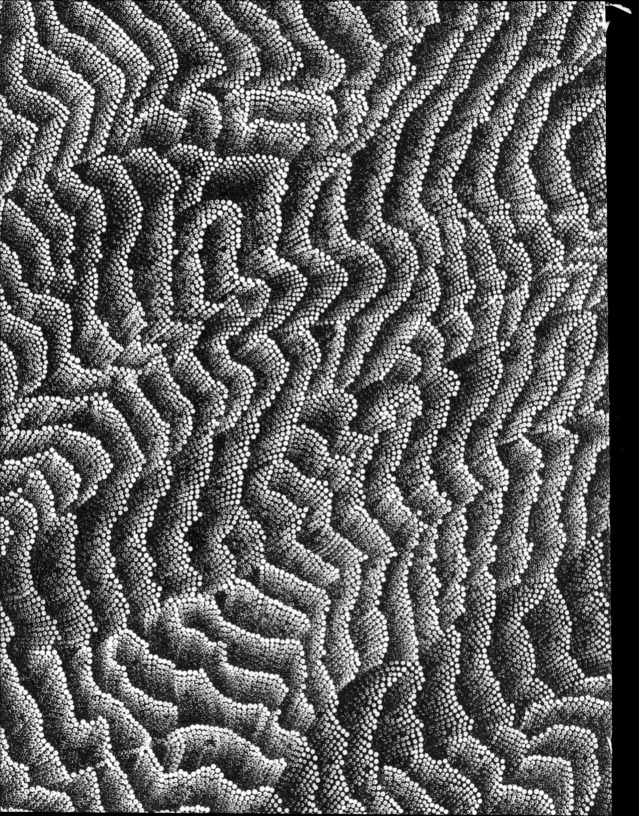